Neville Southall
The Biography of An Everton Legend

Caroline Elwood-Stokes

All Rights Reserved

No part of this book may be reproduced in any form,
by photocopying or by any electronic or mechanical means,
including information storage or retrieval systems,
without permission in writing from both the copyright
owner and the publisher of this book

Copyright 2022 Caroline Elwood-Stokes / John E. Camm

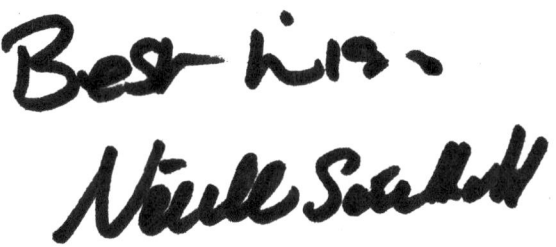

If I die tomorrow, I've had a good life. I'm quite happy. I'm quite peaceful. I don't want to die but I've worked out now that as long as you're comfortable within yourself, death is not really a fear, is it?"

Neville Southall

What can you say about big Nev? Not just a football legend on the pitch but a peoples legend off it.

A brilliant person to be around, intelligent & funny. He has time & patience for everyone, which I find amazing. It's a pleasure being Nevs agent especially after watching him for years following the mighty blues. I hope the book is a massive success. I know I have a friend for life in Nev.

Neville Southall MBE

@davecocky & Mersey memorabilia

Contents

Foreword
Special Thanks
Dedicated to
In memory of
The reason why

Chapter 1:   Trivia Facts
Chapter 1.1: Did you know?
Chapter 2:   Has Nev gotten his car jammed
Chapter 3: The manager gave me a lift home & it was a long way
Chapter 4: Early days at at Everton
Chapter 5: The difficult second season
Chapter 6: Can you guarentee me a clean sheet?
Chapter 7: Going to Wembley twice
Chapter 8: You've had your turn, haven't you?
Chapter 9: Why didn't you catch it?
Chapter 10: Munich and beyond
Chapter 11: The ban
Chapter 12: The sort of player who wins championships
Chapter 13: The Harvey years
Chapter 14: Three transfer requests and a protest
Chapter 15: Howards return
Chapter 16: Royle appointment
Chapter 17: The leaving of Everton
Chapter 18: Life after Goodison
Chapter 19: Neville on...
Chapter: 20: Making the world a better place
Chapter: 21: Build a rapport, treat them like adults
Chapter: 22: I'm basically a nugget
Chapter: 23: I think we fight too much to feel good
Chapter: 24: Accelerated in the last decade
Chapter: 25: Any member of your family could be doing it
Chapter: 26: You dreamed of being a professional footballer

Chapter: 27: That's why I've got a real problem with the LGBT thing
Chapter: 28: You're asking me?
Chapter: 29: Famous quotes
Chapter: 30: Practical Joker
Chapter: 31: Timeline

References

Foreword

"I like when I ask questions and I don't want to find stuff out. I want the answers straight away, I don't want to be waiting for hours and hours and hours.

So Twitter suited me down to the ground because within five seconds normally somebody came back and gave me an answer. It might not always be the answer I like but I always got an answer and I think I like that side of it.

For me to move from football into doing what I'm doing now, I think it's because I got to talk to people I never talked to in my life had I stayed in football"

Neville Southall on why he uses Twitter

This was to be a stress-free, relaxed day in Carmarthen, Wales, for this legend, who was arguably the world's best goalkeeper in the 1980s, as he takes a break from his consuming travelling.

Southall listens while it is explained that our interview will be like no other that he has taken part in. It would be conducted in two halves. John would discuss the football side of stuff and I would be asking random every day to day questions and we settle down for one of the most exhaustive and unusual conversations we've ever had.

Special Thanks

We would like to thank Neville Southall, the legend himself, for agreeing to let us loose on his life. It's a dream come true for us as authors being able to write about a person with the same passions as ourselves. The work Neville does is paramount in this day and age and it's amazing to be able to share that with the world.

We also want to thank to @davecocky & Mersey memorabilia (www.merseymemorabilia.com) for helping to set the book up.. We seriously want your job.

We also want to thank Dave Thomas from the Torbay Weekly for helping us with our research.

We would like to thank Brian Wilkinson for his insights and our friends and family who have been patient enough to let us carry out the research for the book.

We also want to thank everyone who has supported us in the research.

Special thank you to our fans who read our books.

Dedicated to..

Neville Southall, described as one of the greatest goalkeepers of his generation, rightfully deserves the title of an Everton and Wales legend.

In memory of:

Former player and coach Terry Darracott who passed away at the age of 71. Terry was an incredibly popular figure in the game and will be sorely missed by everyone who knew him. Our thoughts are with Terry's family and friends."

Also in memory of 1960s wing-half George Sharples, distinguished scout Bob Pendleton and Lady Rita Carter, the wife of pioneering former Everton Chairman, the late Sir Philip Carter, who died aged 95.

The reason why

On February 22, 2019, a new centre for victims of domestic violence opened in Birkenhead to honour the memory of Paul Lavelle, a fanatical Everton supporter who had been a long-suffering, silent victim of abuse, culminating in his death at the hands of his girlfriend in May 2017.

Attending the unveiling is a corpulent figure, casually attired in a tracksuit top, a blue football shirt and shorts. He delivers a poignant message whilst unveiling the plaque in commemoration of Paul, in front of his close friends and family, who are visibly moved by his presence and touched that this man has taken such a personal interest in their project.

This is not a red-carpet venue where you would expect to find celebrities vying for attention whilst craving tabloid headlines. Yet one man has taken a personal interest in the project out of genuine conviction rather than the opportunity to post an Instagram selfie.

This person is Neville Southall, an Everton and Wales legend who, in the period from 1984 to 1987, was arguably the best goalkeeper in the world.

Chapter 1
Trivia Facts

Name: Neville Southall (French origin that means New Town. Originally a habitational surname for those who came from "the new town" or were new to the town).
Date of Birth: Tuesday, 16 September 1958
Nationality: Welsh
Parents: Fred and Rose Southall
Siblings: One older brother, One younger brother Jeffrey Southall

Relationship Status: Married
Children: Samantha Southall, who is now a mum, (and hates people brushing thier teeth in front of her), Samantha is an Evertonian. Neville also has 2 other orphan children

Religion: Christianity

Birthstone: Sapphire, Lapis Lazuli (The name sapphire is derived from the Latin "saphirus" and the Greek "sapheiros", both of which mean blue. Does this subconciously mean Neville was born an Evertonian?)
Tropical zodiac: Sign Virgo
               Stone: Carnelian
Chinese Zodiac Sign: Earth Dog

Birth flowers: Aster, (mainly symbols of powerful love) and Morning Glory (symbols of affection)

Lucky numbers: Personality Number - 5
                 Life Path - 3

Height: 6 ft 1
Weight: 185 lb / 84 kg
Hair Colour: Brown
Eye Colour: Brown

Foot: Right
House: Living in his own house
Source of Income: Soccer Player
Net Worth: $1.7 Million

Favourite beverage: Tee total (he refuses to drink alcoholic drinks and promotes this kind of behavior.)
Movies: Sharknado 3: Oh Hell No!
TV Shows: The Match

Caps: 92   (W32 D19 L41 GF 108 GA 126 - %45.11)
Goals conceded: 123 (% 1.34 per match)

Age First Cap: 23 yr 253 d   27.5.82 v Northern Ireland 3-0
Age Last Cap: 38 yr 338 d   20.8.97 v Turkey 4-6
National Team Career: 15 yr 85 d

Yellow Cards: 5
Red Cards: 2

Chapter 1.1
Did you know?

Take a look at these fascinating facts about Everton's and Wales all-time great.

- Neville has to take a picture of his car number plate as he can never remember it.
- It's fair to say Neville wasn't exactly a saint – He once went to the kitman when he were on tour in Sweden, and when he saw there was no kit he just walked out in his boots, gloves and underpants. Problem was, he'd not anticipated that there'd be a crowd of people there watching them.
- Yet, not being able to drive meant that Neville was reliant on others for lifts. In a classic Alf Tupper moment was late for one game, arriving at half-time as the train he was travelling on suffered a delay after a brick was thrown through a window.
- Neville Southall amassed 578 appearances during 17 years with the club. At his peak, he was arguably the best in the world.
- Neville studied for an education qualification in Canterbury while managing Hastings United
- Southall will always be remembered as the goalkeeper who went on strike during a match. He sat on the pitch with his back resting against a goalpost with his Everton team trailing 2-0 against Leeds on the opening day of the 1990-1991 season.
- People often regarded Southall as bonkers. He took a pay cut to abandon hod-carrying for the chance of a football career with Bury
- Neville didn't bother checking pay details when he signed for Everton.
- He joined Southend with no idea of the town's location.
- His hatred of football's celebrity circuit, celebration banquets and bling saw him branded a loner.

- Neville once snubbed an Everton FA Cup-winning celebration banquet, preferring to leave Wembley quietly and drive home on his own.
- Southall left school at 16 with no qualifications
- Just 15 months after working as a hod carrier Southall was launched on a 16-year Goodison career.
- Neville does a lot of work within a school in Ebbw Vale helping young people who have come from troubled backgrounds which have been excluded from mainstream schools.
- Neville Southall was voted FWA Footballer of the Year in 1985, making him the last goalkeeper to be given the award.
- Neville Southall is named on the Gwladys Street's Hall of Fame.
- Southall's first cap came against Northern Ireland at the Racecourse Ground, Wrexham on 27 May 1982 in the 1982 British Home Championship, Wales won 3–0.
- Neville won 92 caps between 1982 and 1998, though he did not feature in any major international competitions.
- As an individual, he was named on the PFA Team of the Year four consecutive times.
- He was listed as one of the world's top ten goalkeepers by the International Federation of Football History & Statistics on four occasions.
- He has been named as one of the 100 'Greatest Players of the 20th Century' by World Soccer magazine.
- In the 1996 Birthday Honours, he was appointed a Member of the Order of the British Empire (MBE) for his services to football.
- Neville Southall supports the LGBT community and their rights and sets up charity events for the community often.
- Neville has organized charity events for sex workers and suicide bereavement.

- Big Nev has won more medals for Everton than any other player
- At the age of 41 years and 178 days he became the fourth oldest player in Premier League history
- Neville would wear cheap plastic boots when he played in the rain because they did not retain water.
- Neville would turn up at away games hours before his team-mates so he could familiarise himself with his surroundings
- One of Nev's favourite wind-ups came when Martin Keown joined Everton in 1989. They were going to the Far East for 10 days on a summer tour and Pat Nevin and Nev told him: "It's great when you're away because the club pay your mortgage for you, they get someone to go round and cut your grass and wash your car, you must surely have had that in your contract." Martin was going, "No, no" so Nev told him to go and see Colin Harvey, their manager. Martin knocked on Colin's door, and needless to say, he got pretty short shrift.

Chapter 2
Has Nev gotten his car jammed

Neville was born in the 'Queen of the Welsh Watering Places'. Llandudno is a seaside resort, town, and community in Conwy County Borough, Wales, located on the Creuddyn Peninsula, which protrudes into the Irish sea.

Wales was the only place to go when John and I arranged to meet the man himself. We booked into the Boars Head hotel in Carmarthen, 14 miles from the beautiful Burry Port, west of Llanelli and south-east of Kidwelly, the day before we were due to meet Nev.

Neville was educated at Ysgol John Bright, a secondary school on Maesdu Road, Llandudno. It was founded with money and support from the social reformer John Bright, whose son died in Llandudno in 1864. Until 1969, the school was a selective grammar school known as John Bright grammar school. It reopened in September 1969 as a comprehensive with a new name – Ysgol John Bright.

I'm not sure if it was typical fashion, but John and I were left sitting in an empty function room that smelled like shellfish. It was quite ironic that Nev still hadn't arrived for our arranged meeting in what would be the first half of a match.

Nev's agent informed us that Nev would be with us within 10 minutes. Thank fuck for that. We actually wondered if Nev had gotten his car jammed in the alleyway leading to the car park.

After 10 minutes, the huge heavy doors flung open, and a guy appeared to tell us Nev was here. I stood up with John and ran across the room to the guy, flinging my arms around him, more out of excitement than to greet him. He hugged me back and shook John's hand.

Southall's extraordinary story starts with his dad, Fred, who lied about his age to join the Paratroops and ended up wounded at Arnhem, aged just 21 in 1944. The retired legend describes his dad as "a man's man," saying, "once you've been to war, it must give you a different perspective on life."

Neville didn't have an easy childhood as he was forced to work and play football. Aspiring to be a postman, Neville didn't believe that he would make a living playing football. As a schoolboy, he played in goal for the Caernarfon District side and turned out for Llandudno Swifts in the local Sunday league, competing against adults twice his age.

Nev was working seven days a week whilst turning out for a local non-league side, Bangor City. With Bangor being 20 miles away from Llandudno, Southall relied upon his father to transport him, although on one occasion he forgot to collect him and, with no public transport available, the keeper had to sleep in the stadium itself.

Neville worked as a binman, a waiter, and a hod carrier. He wasn't making more than £10 from football. But as he progressed, he managed to sign contracts that made him rich enough to manage his family and support them financially. Nev talked about how being a footballer, you end up living in a bubble. He had worked a normal life and that gave him a decent grounding and allowed him to do what he wanted to do without giving a fuck.

He went on to explain his days as a bin man and said how the bins taught him that rich people are dirty fuckers and how they would throw away stuff that still worked. He'd pick up big radios that were no use to them but could be useful to someone else. He'd go to building sites and work for his money. I wasn't sure whether to agree or disagree when Nev said footballers don't, but when he continued with "Footballers work for what they can do, not what they do."

I had to agree. There is a big difference. You get paid by the size of the steps in the house, and the sooner you crack on and get the job done, you get paid for the success. Basically, footballers are paid for failure!

Nev would sometimes go into work on his own on a Saturday morning and again on Sunday so he could get ahead. It gave him a good base and he would smash the weekends. So it gives good ground for working harder.
I totally understood Nev's early working life a lot better.

I asked him if he would encourage youths to follow their dream of playing professional football. "Yeah, because they can become millionaires by the age of 20," he answered. I wanted to know if the money was worth the hassle that comes with such a career. Would the money harm a young player? Nev rightly said that money is not the issue; it's what people do with it that counts, and how it affects them as a person. "But can you have too much money too soon?" "Yeah, you can, but not everyone has the same problem," he said with passion in his voice.

Some players use the money wisely, some just get pissed and spend it on fucking speedboats when they live in a flat.

I guess what Nev is saying is that everyone is different. So, we knew much about Neville, and now it was time for him to get to know John and I. He certainly wasn't prepared for what we had in store for him throughout the interview.

I gave him the letter my five-year-old daughter had written for him. "Nev, I love you and mom. "You and mom are on the same team," finished with a drawing of Nev and I playing football. The drawing certainly eased any nerves we had. Nev said I looked like Cher and joked that maybe the image of me was actually meant to be him. Nev was becoming cheeky, but I was loving his sense of humour.

He asked about my children. I explained that I gave birth to three of them and my wife gave birth to the other two.

Chapter 3
The manager gave me a lift home & it was a long way

Neville's football career began at the age of twelve when he joined local side Llandudno Swifts, who were run by his uncle. He would play in both the junior sides and the reserves and also turned out for a local pub team. When he was fifteen, he joined Llandudno Town, who played at a higher level than the Swifts. The following year, he was spotted by Bangor City.

At that time, Bangor competed in the English pyramid system and were in the Northern Premier League. The sixteen-year-old Neville wasn't playing much first team football and was relying on his dad to pick him up from training. He soon moved on to Conwy United, which was much closer to home. His performances at Conwy earned him a trial with Cheshire League side Winsford United. The standard of football was much higher than he'd been used to, but he found that he was equal to it.

In his first season there, Winsford won the league and the Cheshire Senior Cup, with Neville picking up both the Player of the Year and Young Player of the Year awards. In 1980, former Coventry City full back George Rooney was appointed manager of Winsford United. He was told that Neville would be sold to a Football League club to raise vital funds. In an article which appeared on Toffee Web, Rooney later recalled, "I inherited Neville as my goalkeeper, but I was told prior to taking the Winsford job that it had been agreed to sell Neville to Wigan Athletic for a one-off payment of £10,000.

Then I took a call from the Bury manager, Dave Connor. He told me that he would love to sign Neville, but he could only get together £6,000 for a transfer fee. Thinking of where the boy would make the most progress, the big plus about Bury was that their first-choice keeper, John Forrest, was thirty-two and wanted to retire. He had only been playing on as a favour to Dave Connor. "Neville only had to do a decent pre-season at Bury and he would quickly become the first-choice keeper."

"So I decided that that would be the best way for Neville to make a success for himself in the game. I explained to Nev and his dad that Bury was a much better step up the ladder than Wigan, where they already had two established Fourth Division keepers. Neville would have been 3rd choice there and would have to have spent a long time fighting his way through from the "stiffs".
"I told the Winsford chairman, and he said, 'Oh no, I have agreed a deal with Freddie Pye at Wigan. George, you have to see all this through.'

The next week, I had to attend an emergency board meeting at Winsford United with only one thing on the agenda – and that was the sale of Neville Southall to Wigan Athletic for a one-off payment of £10,000! In the meantime, I had managed to get Dave Connor and the Bury Secretary together and they had agreed to pay £6,000 plus VAT (the irony was that Winsford were not VAT-registered, so it brought the fee to nearly £7,000) plus 33% of any future sell-on fee to another club.

I received a phone call from Howard Kendal, the manager of Blackburn Rovers who, at the time, was hotly tipped to become the next manager of Everton, where he had spent much of his playing career. I knew that Howard was originally very keen on taking Neville to Blackburn, but then he cooled off on it. "

"Neville duly signed for Bury and I then attended the hastily put together board meeting in Winsford. I was invited to address the meeting with my manager's report. So, I stood up and said: "Well, gentlemen, the first thing that I have to say is that Neville is not going to Wigan for £10,000. This afternoon he signed for Bury for £6,000 plus VAT. " The room just erupted! I remember the vice-chairman saying to me: "You what? If he is as good as we think he is, you are a bloody fool, Mr. Manager. He could get run down by a bus tomorrow and we'll have lost out on 4,000 quid. "

A month later, I was dismissed from Winsford for allegedly failing to control my players! "Dear Dave, Connor stuck rigidly to his word and Neville started that next season as Bury's first team keeper."

At first, Neville had been reluctant to speak to Dave Connor. They were first introduced by the previous Winsford manager, John Williams. Neville didn't want to speak to Connor because he had to make his way back from a game at Winsford to his home in Llandudno and was concerned that he'd miss his train. Connor countered this by offering to drive Neville to Llandudno, a distance of over 60 miles. This impressed Neville so much that he decided that he wanted to sign for Bury without even discussing wages!

He was approached personally by a representative from Wigan, but his mind was made up. When he did get round to learning about his wages at Bury, it turned out that it would actually be less than he was earning from hod carrying and playing for Winsford He found it a bit of a dilemma deciding whether or not to gamble on a career as a professional footballer, but eventually decided to give it a go.

However, a fortnight before Neville was due to start pre-season training at Bury, Dave Connor was sacked from his role as manager. Neville told me, "The only reason I signed for Bury really was that the manager gave me a lift home and it was a long way! I thought, 'If he's prepared to put himself out like that, then I'll sign for him.' And to be fair, I did get offered a council house if I signed for Wigan the day after, but I'd already made my mind up to sign for Dave Connor. Unfortunately, by the time I got to Bury, he'd been sacked. That's the way it goes. I was walking into somewhere new and I had no idea how professional football worked.

It was a bit of a shock because I didn't think it was that good and the person who signed me up was no longer there, so it was difficult in a way because I didn't know what to expect. And they'd promised to find me a house, but when I called them about it, they told me to go and find one myself! I didn't know the area. I had no idea. I was lucky to be fair because I stayed at one of the lad's houses for the first few weeks of pre-season.

But even then, when I had a day off, I went back to carrying on the building sites because my wages were shit! "

The man chosen to replace Connor was Jim Iley, a stereotypical straight-talking Yorkshireman. John Forrest was still at the club at the time and was still regarded as the first choice goalkeeper, but was at the end of his career. He had become a firm favourite with the fans, having made over 400 first team appearances. Neville was initially to have made his first-team debut in a Fourth Division fixture against Mansfield Town but had to pull out due to illness.

He eventually made his debut against fellow Lancastrians Wigan Athletic on September 20th, 1980. Neville remembers how when he ran out for the warm-up he was booed and verbally abused by Bury supporters who were loyal to Forrest & didn't trust this young upstart in goal! However, he put in a good performance in a 2-1 victory for Bury.

One decision made by Iley which Neville believes had a positive impact on his career was bringing in Wilf McGuinness as coach. McGuinness both played for and managed Manchester United, and he would take Neville for one-on-one training sessions, which he found enormously beneficial. Not only did he learn from McGuiness's specialist coaching and advice, but he also gained a lot of confidence from his infectious personality. Despite playing in a struggling side, Neville was progressing well in the world of professional football. Bury finished the season in mid-table.

Their more memorable moments came in the cup competitions. They beat Newcastle in the League Cup before going out to European Champions Nottingham Forest in the third round, losing to Fulham in a second replay. They also made it to the semi-finals of the now defunct Anglo-Scottish Cup in what was to be its final year, losing to eventual winners, Chesterfield. Neville had kept fifteen clean sheets in forty-four games and was rumoured to have caught the eye of clubs like Manchester United and Chelsea.

There was then newspaper speculation that Everton were interested but that there was a problem with the deal because Winsford would be owed 25% of the fee. Although they had agreed to this a year earlier when they'd signed Neville, it now seemed that Bury were hoping to avoid paying it and instead offered to pay just £10,000.00 out of a £150,000 transfer fee. Winsford chairman, Cliff Noden, was understandably unhappy about this, and it seemed the deal had been called off and that Neville would instead be moving to Newcastle. Eventually, however, following heated exchanges between Noden and Bury chairman Ron Clarke, Winsford agreed to accept a payment of £25,000 and on July 7th, 1981, Neville became an Everton player. Despite his relatively short stay at Bury, Neville always held the club close to his heart and, years later, he was very supportive of the Shakers in their ultimately unsuccessful battle against expulsion from the Football League.

Chapter 4
Early days at at Everton

In May 1981, Howard Kendall, who already enjoyed legendary status among the Goodison Park faithful following his time there as a player, replaced Gordon Lee as Everton manager. Prior to this, Kendall had led Blackburn Rovers to promotion to the second division in 1980 and the following season, only goal difference had kept them from promotion to the top tier.

On arriving at the club, one of Kendall's priorities was to sign a goalkeeper. He'd been aware of Neville since his time at Winsford United, following a chance meeting with Neville's father in a bar in Llandudno. Kendall had been to watch Neville play and was impressed by what he saw and had first attempted to sign him for Blackburn Rovers in the summer of 1980.

Liverpool in the summer of 1981 was very different from the quiet towns of Ramsbottom or Llandudno, where Neville had lived previously. The city had been ravaged by the infamous Toxteth riots, which saw violent clashes between the police and members of the local black community. It was certainly a bit of a culture shock for the young goalkeeper.

He was, however, immediately impressed by the club and by Howard Kendall, whom he described as "a decent fellow and a bundle of energy." Kendall offered to double the wages that he was receiving from Bury. He also offered to take Neville out for a few drinks and seemed to find it hard to believe that he had just signed a teetotaller!

Kendall's right-hand man at Everton was Colin Harvey, a native of the city who, despite his friendly, mild-mannered personality, took on a much more aggressive and demanding demeanour on the training ground. He'd been the same during his playing days with Everton and Sheffield Wednesday. He led by example, always giving 100% while joining in with training himself, and Neville was impressed by this approach. He constantly demanded more from the players but was always willing to quietly give one-on-one advice where he felt it would be beneficial. Harvey and his honest, hardworking attitude rubbed off on Neville and had a positive impact on his career.

When Neville arrived at Everton, they already had two experienced goalkeepers on their books. One was Republic of Ireland international Jim McDonagh, who had been signed by previous manager Gordon Lee a year earlier. McDonagh had become a highly respected keeper, enjoying several successful seasons at Bolton Wanderers before eventually joining Everton. The other was Jim Arnold, who Kendall had brought with him from Blackburn for a fee of £200'000.

Arnold had spent much of his career in non-league football with Stafford Rangers before making his football league debut at the relatively late age of 29, after Kendall had signed him for Blackburn. He'd kept a club record of 19 clean sheets during Blackburn's 1979/80 promotion campaign and was clearly highly rated by Kendall.

It was a time of change at Goodison Park. Also added to the squad by Kendall were Mick Walsh, a tough, old-style centre half; winger Mickey Thomas; and strikers Mick Ferguson and Alan Biley. Out went full back John Gidman and England striker Bob Latchford.

When the 1981/82 season began, Jim Arnold was the first choice goalkeeper. This was to be expected as he was more experienced than Neville and had done an excellent job for Howard Kendall at Blackburn. Neville began the season in the reserve team. At the time, Kendall was still registered as a player and also played in the reserves.

Neville soon realised that at this level, you really had to take responsibility for your own career. Being shy by nature meant that he didn't speak to a lot of people at the club. He didn't go out drinking with the other players, which is when many of them tended to bond. Kendall would invite him for a drink in the early days, but soon came to realise that it just wasn't going to happen.

Neville made his first team debut for Everton on October 17th, 1981 in a home game against Ipswich Town. Jim Arnold had an injury & an hour before kick off, Kendall simply said to Neville, "By the way, you're playing." This gave Neville very little time to feel nervous, but also meant that there was no time for his usual preparation. Neville found the Everton fans more supportive of a young debutant goalkeeper than some of those at Bury. The Toffees won 2-1 thanks to goals from Mick Ferguson and Gary Stevens.

Neville's best moment was a good save from Eric Gates. However, the following week, Jim Arnold had recovered from injury and reclaimed his first team spot, and it wouldn't be until a few days before Christmas that Neville would get another chance. Everton had been knocked out of the League Cup by Ipswich & unhappy with the performance, Howard Kendall had shown a more ruthless side to his character by dropping Ferguson, Biley, Walsh, Eamonn O'Keefe &, significantly for Neville, Jim Arnold, for a home game against reigning league champions Aston Villa.

Everton won the game 2-0 and Neville would go on to keep the number one jersey for the rest of the season, which saw Everton eventually finish in 8th place.
During his first season at Goodison Park, Neville came to realise that Howard Kendall wasn't a man to heap praise on his players. He recalled how, in the early days, he'd come back into the dressing room feeling that he'd played well only for Kendall to be critical of a decision that he'd

made at some point during the match. When, after several first team games, this stopped happening so often, Neville took it to mean that Kendall was satisfied with his performances.

He also found that Kendall was happy for him to do things his own way, providing it was for the good of the team. As Neville was single-mindedly aiming to be the best goalkeeper that he could possibly be, Kendall was happy to let him do things his own way. This would, after all, benefit the team as a whole. Kendall, however, never guaranteed Neville that he was first choice.

He was apparently only chosen for the first team slot on a match-by-match basis. Neville assumed this was simply to keep him on his toes and ensure that he kept working hard. Plus, he had stiff competition from Jim Arnold. Also at the club was Martin Hodge, who, after recovering from a particularly bad knee injury, went on to have a successful career which included playing 214 consecutive games for Sheffield Wednesday.

There was never any animosity between the keepers. During the 1981/82 season, Hodge was working hard to recover from his injury. Arnold and Neville would train together and get on well. Despite this, Neville was well aware that he had to stay at his very best to stop Arnold from reclaiming his place.

Chapter 5
The difficult second season

During the summer of 1982, it became clear that Howard Kendall wasn't entirely happy with his squad of players. Alan Biley & Mickey Thomas left the club while Mick Ferguson, Mike Walsh & Alan Ainscow had fallen out of favour & would soon follow.

By the end of the 1981/82 season, Graeme Sharp, a Scottish striker who previous manager Gordon Lee had signed from Dumbarton, and Gary Stevens, a right back who was a product of the club's youth system, had broken into the first team. Adrian Heath, a 21-year old striker, was signed by Stoke City for a club record fee of £850,000. Club captain Mike Lyons moved to Sheffield on Wednesday.

In came David Johnson & Kevin Sheedy from local rivals Liverpool & former Goodison favourite Andy King was signed from West Bromwich Albion for a second spell with the club.

When the season had finished, most of the players went on an end-of-season holiday abroad. This didn't interest teetotal Neville. All he wanted to do was play and didn't enjoy the summer break. He carried on training and, as a result, he was still at full fitness when pre-season began. The 1982/83 season got off to a bad start for the Toffees when they were beaten 2-0 by Graham Taylor's newly promoted Watford side at Vicarage Road.

The following match was a home game against reigning European Champions Aston Villa, which Everton won 5-0. This was followed by a comfortable 3-1 victory over Tottenham at Goodison Park. Indifferent form followed until November 6th, when local rivals Liverpool were the visitors to Goodison Park. It was to be a day which Neville came to remember as one of the worst of his long career. Liverpool were already a goal in front when, after 30 minutes, Glenn Keeley, who had been brought in on loan from Blackburn by Howard Kendall, was sent off for a professional foul on Kenny Dalglish.

At the beginning of the season, it had been announced that a deliberate foul on a player in a clear goal-scoring position would result in a straight red card for the perpetrator. Keeley, who had been out injured all season, later claimed that he had no knowledge of this, but the damage was done. Liverpool would go on to win 5-0 and there were bound to be repercussions for the Everton team.

Publicly, Howard Kendall tried to play down the result, pointing out that they were beaten by arguably the best side in Europe while playing for all but the first 30 minutes with 10 men on the field. Behind closed doors, however, he was far from happy. Neville had been suffering from ulcerated toes, which had become increasingly painful. After the match, he was sent to the hospital, which meant that he missed much of the fallout from the defeat.

Kendall reacted by dropping Brian Borrows, Kevin Sheedy, John Bailey, and Keeley. It turned out that the 30 minutes he played in that game would be his only appearance for Everton. Although technically injured after the Liverpool game, Neville was also a casualty of Kendall's changes & Jim Arnold was reinstated as first choice goalkeeper.

In those days, there was only one substitute allowed, which meant no place on the bench for the second choice keeper. Neville was expected to be there on match days in case Jim Arnold couldn't play for any reason, but the only games he was playing in were reserve matches. Often, second XI fixtures were played on a Saturday and so, with him having to be with the first team, he missed them.

It was not an ideal situation from Neville's point of view. He just wanted to play and was finding the boredom hard to cope with. He refused to give up on his Everton career and trained hard in the hope that another chance would come. Things then took an unexpected turn for him a couple of months after the Liverpool defeat.

He was called into Howard Kendall's office and told that Fourth Division Port Vale wanted him to join them on loan. Due to their regular number one, Barry Siddall, suffering a knee injury, Neville had no hesitation in accepting the offer to play first team football. The fact that it'd mean dropping down the leagues didn't matter. It was a chance to get back to doing what he loved.

Neville enjoyed his time at Port Vale. He made nine appearances, including a 1-0 win away at his old club Bury, in a team which would go on to finish third with 88 points and win promotion. At the end of his two-month loan spell, Vale manager John McGrath attempted to sign him on a permanent basis, but the bid was rejected by Howard Kendall, so Neville returned to Goodison Park and the role of backup goalkeeper. Everton were in the top half of the First Division and also managed to reach the quarter-finals of the FA Cup, where they lost 1-0 to Manchester United.

United progressed to the final, where they beat Brighton & Hove Albion in a replay.

With four games of the 1982/83 season left to play, an injury to Jim Arnold meant that Neville was finally recalled to the first team. He returned for a 2-0 home victory over West Ham, followed by wins against Coventry & Luton and a draw at home to Ipswich. To Neville, it was a satisfactory end to what had been a difficult season.

Chapter 6
Can you guarantee me a clean sheet?

The beginning of the 1983/84 season saw Jim Arnold fit again and back in possession of the number one jersey. Neville accepted this. He believed that as long as he carried on working hard, his chance would come again. During the summer, Howard Kendall signed winger Trevor Steven from Burnley and Alan Harper, who could play in virtually any outfield position, from Liverpool, where he had failed to break into the first team. Out went Steve McMahon, who joined Aston Villa.

The season didn't start well with only 2 wins in the first 7 matches, and pressure was beginning to mount on Kendall with the Goodison crowd becoming increasingly restless. On the 1st of October, he made the decision to play Neville in goal for a game against Notts County at Meadow Lane. A 33rd minute goal by Peter Reid was enough to ensure that Everton returned home to Merseyside with all three points.

Neville kept his place in the first team, but indifferent form continued, however, with wins over Watford and Nottingham Forest being the only successes during the next 7 games. In November, concerned by a lack of goals, Kendall signed Scotland international striker Andy Gray from Wolves. He had been a prolific goalscorer at Molineaux as well as at his previous clubs, Aston Villa and Dundee United. Gray was a quality player who was very vocal and demanded high standards from those around him. This was to have a positive effect on the team as a whole and he soon formed a formidable partnership with fellow Scottish striker Graeme Sharp.

December began with a victory over Manchester United, and Gray scored the lone goal against his former club Villa. This, though, was followed by a run of four goalless games for the Toffees & large sections of the Everton crowd were venting their frustration towards Howard Kendall. His garage was vandalised when the words "Kendall out" were painted on it & some fans were handing out leaflets before games demanding his removal. Neville tried to ignore what was happening around him and concentrate solely on what he had to do. He has since wondered whether this could be regarded as selfish, but, as always, he was single-mindedly focused on doing his job to the best of his ability.

His view was that he couldn't be up front scoring goals or passing the ball around the midfield. He could, however, stop goals from being conceded. That was, after all, his role in the team. Neville remembers an incident when the strain started to show on the normally placid Kendall.

Everton had a New Year's Eve fixture at home to Coventry City. Kendall was fearing that defeat would lead to him being sacked. During a training session a couple of days before the match, Kendall approached Neville and asked, "Can you guarantee me a clean sheet against Coventry?" It was a silly question because there are a seemingly infinite number of possible scenarios which leave a goalkeeper in a position where he can do nothing to stop a goal being conceded.

Neville replied, "No, I can't." Kendall then went over to Jim Arnold and asked him the same question. Like Neville, Arnold told him that he couldn't. A goalless draw meant that Kendall kept his job and Neville kept his place.
If Everton's league form had been disappointing, the cup competitions were bringing some welcome relief.

Victories over Chesterfield, Coventry, West Ham & Oxford United meant that in February, Everton faced Aston Villa over two legs in the semi final of the League Cup, or Milk Cup, as it was also known between 1981 & 1986 due to a sponsorship deal with the Milk Marketing Board. Unlike today, when the cup competitions are regarded as little more than an annoying distraction by the bigger clubs, all competitions were taken very seriously & full strength sides were fielded.

Consequently, Neville had played in every match up to the semi-final. Andy Gray was cup tied for the competition, having played for Wolves in earlier rounds. A clean sheet from Neville and goals from Kevin Sheedy and Kevin Richardson gave Everton a 2-0 lead to take into the second leg at Villa Park, where a 1-0 win for Villa wasn't enough to stop Everton progressing to the final at Wembley, where they were to face their neighbours and rivals from the other side of Stanley Park, Liverpool.

Chapter 7
Going to Wembley twice

On the 25th March 1984, Neville walked onto a rain-drenched pitch for his first Wembley final. It was also the first all-Merseyside cup final & the teams were met by an almost deafening roar as they emerged from the tunnel, which in the old stadium was located behind the east goal.

Everton could consider themselves unlucky in the first half when Alan Hansen handled a goal-bound Adrian Heath shot only for the referee, Alan Robinson, to ignore appeals for a penalty. A decision in Everton's favour would also have almost certainly resulted in a red card for Hansen.

Neville would later acknowledge that while it was fair to say that Hansen had been lucky, Kevin Richardson had also escaped justice for a similar incident during the semi-final against Villa. Neville's first major contribution to the final came when a dive to his right stopped a long-range effort from Graeme Souness. He would later make saves from Ronnie Whelan, Kenny Dalglish and Ian Rush. The Toffees would also have a lucky escape when Rush somehow managed to scoop the ball over the bar from close range when a goal seemed certain. The match went to extra time and, after both Whelan and Alan Kennedy had put the ball into Neville's net only to be denied by the offside flag, remained goalless.

Just 3 days later, a crowd of 52,089 crammed into Manchester City's Maine Road ground to see a largely uneventful replay settled by a 20-yard Graeme Souness strike after 21 minutes. Despite their obvious disappointment, Everton didn't have to wait long for another chance to play in another final beneath the famous twin towers. Just 2 weeks after their League Cup Final appearance, they were to meet Southampton at Arsenal's ground, Highbury, for the semi-final of the FA

Cup. Everton had progressed to this stage with wins over Stoke City, Gillingham (after 2 replays), Shrewsbury Town and Notts County.

Neville dived to his left to make a good save from Saints' striker Steve Moran early on in the game and then produced an excellent stop just before half time when Danny Wallace looked almost certain to score. After the break, it was Wallace again who almost broke the deadlock when he accelerated past the Everton defence only to see Southall's fingertips divert the ball past the post for a corner.

Everton then had a good spell where they piled pressure on the Saints defence and Adrian Heath missed a good chance with only Southampton goalkeeper, Peter Shilton, left to beat. Goalless after 90 minutes, the match went to extra time and Neville got down quickly to his left to deny veteran striker Frank Worthington from putting the South Coast club ahead.

Finally, with just 3 minutes of extra time remaining, Heath, nicknamed "Inchy" due to his short stature, got his head to a Peter Reid free kick and directed it past Shilton to send Everton into the final. Neville's performance had been impressive and earned him some very positive comments on the back pages. His reputation as a goalkeeper was in the ascendancy. More importantly for him and his teammates, Everton were playing in their first FA Cup Final since 1968.

Their opponents would be Watford, who had beaten Third Division Plymouth Argyle in the other semi-final at Villa Park and had finished the previous First Division season as runners-up.

Despite being up against strong opposition, Everton were determined not to fall at the final hurdle as they had in their previous Wembley appearance and confidence was high. Howard Kendall wanted his players to remain relaxed in the build-up to the big game and invited comedian Freddie Starr, who was an Everton supporter, to entertain them at the team hotel on the eve of the match.

In the lead up to the game, much was made in the media of the fact that the Watford chairman was music legend Elton John. Elton's family already had FA Cup history. His paternal cousin, Roy Dwight, had scored for Nottingham Forest against Luton Town in the 1959 final. Watford, at the time renowned for their "long ball" style of play, were managed by Graham Taylor, who six years later would take charge of the England national team.

Neville was called into action in the very first minute when he made a save from a John Barnes header. The Toffees' first chance came when Graeme Sharp headed wide following a Trevor Steven cross from the right. Kevin Richardson then went close before Gary Stevens forced a save out of Steve Sherwood in the Hornets' goal. Neville again saved Barnes. Everton were in front after 38 minutes. A long range attempt from Gary Stevens was blocked but it fell to Sharp, who had the time and space to slot the ball beyond the reach of Sherwood and inside the post.

The first opening of the second half was created by Watford when Neville did well to pluck a Kenny Jackett cross out of the air with Barnes waiting at the far post. Just 6 minutes after the restart, however, Everton got their second.

A Trevor Steven cross was met by the head of Andy Gray as Sherwood reached for the ball. There were claims that Gray had headed the ball out of Sherwood's hands, but the referee, John Hunting, saw no infringement. Watford offered little threat after that. The ball was headed by Mo Johnston, who later in his career would play for Everton, past Neville and into the goal, but the whistle had already been blown for offside. It was Everton's first FA Cup win since 1966 and the first major honour of Neville's career. Despite his delight at winning the trophy, Neville's feelings towards the celebrations demonstrated his grounded approach to his professional career.

He later spoke of how he felt awkward about going up to the Royal Box to collect his medal from the Duchess of Kent and then going on the lap of honour afterwards. He felt the same way about the after-match party and the victory parade around the streets of Liverpool. For him, he was paid to help win football matches, and that was what he'd just done.

Chapter 8
You've had your turn, haven't you?

Between 1982 and 1997, Neville made a total of 92 appearances for the Welsh national side. This makes him his country's fourth most capped player of all time, behind Chris Gunter, Gareth Bale, and fellow goalkeeper Wayne Hennessey. During the early days of his career, Neville says that playing for Wales never really crossed his mind. This could be regarded as surprising given that, in a country where the most popular sport is rugby union, the Welsh have a relatively small pool of players to choose from.

The fact is, though, that he hadn't played for any of the international schoolboy or youth teams and didn't play league football until he was 20 years old, so it hadn't occurred to him that he might eventually be his country's first choice keeper. Even during his time at Bury, he didn't feel sure that he had a future in professional football and didn't rule out a return to hod carrying.

The first time that Neville realised that he was in the thoughts of Wales manager, Mike England, was when he was put on standby for a European Championship qualifier against Turkey, which took place on March 25th, 1981. At the time, he was still playing in the Fourth Division with Bury.

This meant he was third choice keeper & Neville later remarked that the Welsh FA were far too tight on the purse strings to fly him out there when he was almost certain not to be called upon to play! Shortly after joining Everton, he was called up for the first time by Wales, although at that time, the far more experienced Dai Davies was preferred by Mike England.

Neville finally made his international debut in a British Home Championship match against Northern Ireland at Wrexham's Racecourse Ground on May 27th, 1982. The Home Championship was an annual tournament which was contested towards the end of every season between England, Scotland, Wales and Northern Ireland until it was abolished in 1984. Wales won the game 3-0 courtesy of goals from Alan Curtis, Ian Rush, and Peter Nicholas.

Unfortunately, the match coincided with the FA Cup final replay between Queens Park Rangers and Tottenham, with many fans opting to stay at home and watch that instead. As a result, the attendance at the Racecourse Ground was only 2,315. This didn't matter to Neville, though. Not only had he played for his country and kept a clean sheet, he'd played against his goalkeeping hero, Pat Jennings.

A few days later, Wales travelled to France, where they were to play a friendly against the national side on June 2nd at the Stadium Municipal in Toulouse. Disappointingly for Neville, Dai Davies was restored to the side. When he asked Mike England for a reason, the reply was a simple "You've had your turn, haven't you?" It's difficult to argue with! Despite this, Neville both liked and respected Mike England, who, during his playing days, had been a centre half for Blackburn and Tottenham as well as captain of Wales.

England didn't have an easy job working for the Football Association of Wales, who, according to Neville, were at the time both amateurish and always looking for ways to ensure that they spent as little money as possible. As a result, all flights were standard class and hotels were generally poor.

They even changed Mike England's contract from full to part time, cutting his pay by more than 50%! What annoyed Neville was that while the bare minimum was spent on the players and coaching staff, the FAW committee members enjoyed the high life wherever they went. England constantly fought for better conditions for their team, but it always fell on deaf ears.

On September 22nd, 1982, Neville was recalled to the Wales starting XI for a European Championship qualifier against Norway at Swansea City's Vetch Field. He again kept a clean sheet, with an Ian Rush goal being the difference between the sides. From this point on, he would become a regular in the side and, despite the fact that, during his career, Wales didn't qualify for a major tournament, he played in some memorable games. One such match was an unexpected victory over England at Wrexham in May 1984, in what was to be the last British Home Championship. Mark Hughes scored the only goal that day, and Wales finished the tournament as runners-up to Northern Ireland.

One game which he doesn't remember so fondly is a qualifying match for the 1986 Mexico World Cup against Iceland in Reykjavik . At the time, Iceland were considered regarded as one of the weakest teams in Europe & it was a game in which Wales couldn't afford to slip up, with Spain and Scotland being the other teams in the group. Things didn't go to plan though & a 51st minute header from Magnus Bergs was enough to win the game for the home side. Neville tells us how, after the game, Mike England was absolutely furious and laid into his team. "I suppose you fuckers will be going out drinking and all that," he raged. One player quietly pointed out that Mike himself had organised a post-match disco. "All right then, fair play," said England, suddenly calming down.

Being a proud Welshman, though, Neville always considered it an honour to represent his country and, in some ways, enjoyed the fact that the lack of professionalism made it a less intense experience than playing for his club. He also later pointed out that he certainly didn't play international football for the money!

One incident which illustrates how crazy life in the Wales national side could be in the 1980s was when Wales played Iceland at Ninian Park, Cardiff, in November 1984. Amazingly, Wales didn't have the full number of substitutes for the game. Fulham defender Jeff Hopkins wasn't in the squad but had gone to the game as a spectator. Before kick off, he went to the dressing room to wish the team good luck and Mike England asked him if he had his boots.

When Hopkins told him that they were in his car, England said, "Well go and get them then, you're on the bench." After 50 minutes, Hopkins, who hadn't prepared for the game, was sent on in place of Jeremy Charles. As if that wasn't enough, After the game, England ripped into him about his apparent poor performance!

It was while on international duty, however, that Neville experienced one of the saddest days of his career, one which reminds us all that football is, in fact, just a game. Wales' last match of the World Cup 86 qualifiers was against Scotland at Ninian Park on September 10th, 1985. A win for Wales would see them finish top of the group and qualify for Mexico, consigning Spain to the play-offs. Scotland could also qualify by winning, so the stakes were high. Everywhere Scotland went, they were backed by a large and noisy following & this was certainly no exception, with an estimated 12,000 heading to Cardiff.

As part of his pre-match warm-up routine, Neville was having balls kicked at him, but one by one they went into the Scotland crowd, who refused to return them. When he eventually had none left and the Tartan Army still refused to throw them back, he went to find Scotland manager Jock Stein. Stein was one of the legends of Scottish football. He had managed Celtic when, in 1967, they became the first British side to win the European Cup and had also led them to 10 Scottish League Championships in 12 seasons. Neville asked Stein if he would get the fans to return the balls, and, being the gentleman that he was, he duly obliged. Such was the respect for Stein that the balls were thrown back and a grateful Neville carried on with his warmup.

The game, which was being broadcast live across the UK on the ITV network, got off to a frantic start and Wales took the lead after just 13 minutes when Mark Hughes directed a low cross from Peter Nicholas past Jim Leighton. The atmosphere in the stadium was electric with so much at stake and emotions running high. There were even reports of Mike England and FAW General Secretary Alun Evans almost coming to blows outside the Welsh dressing room at half time.

There was a bizarre incident in the Scottish dressing room at half time. It came to light that, during the first half, Scotland goalkeeper Jim Leighton had lost a contact lens. This was particularly surprising to Jock Stein and his assistant Alex Ferguson, who was also Leighton's manager at Aberdeen, as neither of them were aware that he wore contact lenses! It turned out that he'd kept it a secret because he feared it would harm his career. Stein was absolutely furious and, for the second half, replaced Leighton with Hibernian's Alan Rough, for what would be Rough's 52nd and penultimate international cap. Rough remembers that as he left the dressing room, Stein simply said to him, "Good luck, ya fat bastard!"

After the break, Scotland fought hard for an equaliser, but Neville and the Wales defence held firm until, with 9 minutes left to play and with the Welsh seemingly within touching distance of a place at the World Cup in Mexico, the ball struck the arm of David Phillips & Dutch referee Jan Keizer awarded a penalty.

Davie Cooper took the spot kick and hit it low to Neville's left. Neville got a hand to the ball, but it wasn't enough to prevent it from going into the net and shattering Welsh dreams. The last 9 minutes were frantic as Wales tried in vain to restore their lead, but the Scots hung on and would ultimately qualify for Mexico following a 2-0 aggregate win over Australia in a play-off.

The Scottish fans were overjoyed after their team had trailed for so long. However, their joy was about to be brought to an abrupt halt by the events which were unfolding at the side of the pitch. When Scotland equalised, Jock Stein remained seated and unanimated while those around him celebrated, although, shortly afterwards, he remonstrated with a photographer to move out of the way as he was blocking his view of the game.

Two minutes before the end of normal time, the referee blew the whistle for a foul, and it appeared that Stein thought it was the final whistle and began to head towards the Wales bench to shake hands with Mike England. Instead, however, he fell to the ground and was immediately carried to the dressing room, where medical staff fought hard to save him, but there was nothing they could do. Jock Stein was dead at just 62 years of age.

Following another failed attempt to qualify for a major tournament, this time the 1988 European Championships, Mike England was replaced as manager by Terry Yorath, who was still a Wales player when Neville had first joined the team. Neville felt that Mike England had always been treated unfairly by the FAW and didn't deserve to lose his job. However, despite being a very different type of manager to Mike England, Neville thought that Yorath was a good appointment.

He feels that he got the best out of players who had played their club football in the lower leagues. Despite this, the Welsh again missed out on tournament football. To reach the finals of Italia 90, they were unlucky to be drawn in a group containing West Germany & European Champions, Holland, as well as Finland. Wales finished bottom of the group with just two points from their six games, although they did hold the Germans, who went on to become the world champions, to a 0-0 draw.

Wales were again drawn in the same group as West Germany in the qualifying stages of the 1992 European Championships. East Germany was also in the group at the time of the draw, but after the announcement of reunification, Germany became one team and took on West German fixtures.

One match which Neville will always be proud to have been a part of is the game against the Germans at Cardiff Arms Park in June 1991. He had a busy night, as you'd expect against the World Champions, but in the 66th minute, and against the run of play, Ian Rush grabbed the only goal of the game, making it a truly memorable night for Welsh football.

Sadly, however, Wales were to finish second in their group & again miss out on the finals.

When the job of Wales manager became available in 1995, Neville applied. The position instead went to an Englishman, Bobby Gould, who had managed Wimbledon's famous "Crazy Gang." Gould quickly made Neville and Ian Rush his assistants and, although other goalkeepers played in various friendly fixtures, Neville continued to play in competitive games.

His final international appearance came in August 1997 when Gould blamed him for the three first-half goals conceded in a 6-4 defeat against Turkey and substituted him at half time. In 1999, Gould resigned suddenly just four days before Wales were due to play Denmark at Anfield. Neville & Mark Hughes were asked to manage the side for the fixture and duly obliged, with Hughes playing and Neville on the touchline in a match which the Danes won 2-0. Neville applied for the vacant manager's job, but the FAW appointed Hughes instead.

Chapter 9
Why didn't you catch it?

During the summer of 1984, Neville signed a new contract with Everton. He has said that he doesn't believe that the money was as much as many other players were earning at the time, but he liked the security of knowing where he'd be playing for the next 4 years, so he could then just concentrate on the job in hand. Howard Kendall hadn't made many changes to his squad during the summer. The only notable signing was when he brought in midfielder Paul Bracewell from Sunderland.

The 1984–85 season began with another visit to Wembley for the FA Charity Shield (now called the FA Community Shield). As is the tradition, the match was played between the previous season's league champions and FA Cup winners, which meant another game against city rivals Liverpool.

It was Liverpool who had the first clear chance when Neville came rushing out of his goal with Kenny Dalglish bearing down on him, only for Dalglish's shot to fly wide of the post. Everton almost took the lead when a dipping, long-range effort from Adrian Heath brought a superb flying save from Bruce Grobbelaar. Again, Dalglish found himself through on goal, only for Neville to come off his line and block with his legs.

In the second half, Graeme Sharp probably should have done better from close range, but Grobbelaar again saved. The only goal came in bizarre fashion in the 56th minute. Sharp burst through the Liverpool defence. His first shot was stopped by Grobbelaar. The ball came back to him but his second attempt was blocked by Alan Hansen, only for the ball to strike Grobbelaar, who was rushing back towards his goal, on the shins and rebound into the net. It was a good start to the season for the Toffees and went some way towards avenging their League Cup final defeat by their neighbours a few months earlier.

A week later, an expectant crowd of 30,630 turned up at Goodison Park for the first league game of the season at home to Tottenham, only to witness a comfortable 4-1 win for the North London side. This was followed by a 2-1 defeat at West Bromwich Albion. Next up was Chelsea at Stamford Bridge, and a 1-0 victory, courtesy of a Kevin Richardson goal, began a run of 4 wins and 2 draws, which included a thrilling 5-4 win over the previous season's FA Cup final opponents, Watford, at Vicarage Road.

Left back Pat van den Hauwe was signed from Birmingham City for £100,000 & would go on to play a major role in their future successes. This effectively brought about the end of John Bailey's time in the first team, and Neville felt a lot of sympathy for him. He believed that Bailey was a far better player than most people gave him credit for being. He would leave the club in 1986 and continue his career with Newcastle United and Bristol City.

A game which will long be remembered by the Everton faithful was the visit to Anfield on October 20th. During the first half, Neville saved from Ian Rush when the Liverpool striker looked certain to score. The second half was only 3 minutes old when Graeme Sharp scored one of the best goals ever to grace a Merseyside derby when his long-range drive left Grobbelaar clutching at thin air.

Peter Reid almost doubled the lead after a mistake in the Liverpool defence before Neville pushed away a Dalglish free kick. Everton hung on to claim their first win at Anfield for over 14 years. A week later, Manchester United, who at the time were top of the league, were the visitors to Goodison where an outstanding all-round team performance, along with 2 goals from Kevin Sheedy and one each from Adrian Heath, Gary Stevens, and Graeme

Sharp, saw Everton run out 5-0 winners. Neville later said that, to him, the performance was faultless with every team member doing their job.

By this time, there was a confidence in the team which hadn't previously been evident during Neville's time at the club. There was also great team spirit off the pitch, which is important if you want to bring about success off it. A 3-0 home win over Leicester City at the beginning of November saw Everton go top of the league & that was pretty much where they'd stay for the rest of the season. Following on from some lean times & all the pressure being piled on Howard Kendall, crowds were now turning up at Goodison expecting to see the home side win.

Neville found that sometimes it was difficult to concentrate on what he had to do among all the euphoria off the pitch He avoided the media and just thought about the next match.

Everton's FA Cup final win saw them rewarded with more than just getting to keep the famous old trophy for a year. It also gave them a place in the European Cup Winner's Cup. This was, as the name suggests, a knock-out competition competed for by the winners of each European nation's premier domestic cup competition and was in existence from 1960 to 1999. Ties were played over 2 legs except for the final, which was played at a neutral venue.

In the first round, Everton were drawn against part-timers, University College Dublin (known as UCD) and were expected to progress to the next round without any difficulty. Neville described them as "a student team basically." To give you some idea of the difference between the clubs, UCD had only turned from amateur to semi-professional during the previous year. One fan, when asked why he attended UCD matches, replied, "Because I don't like crowds!" Despite all this, UCD held Everton to a goalless draw in the first leg in front of almost 10,000 people, which was many times more than their average attendance. In the return leg at Goodison Park, Graeme Sharp put Everton ahead, but UCD clipped Neville's crossbar in the closing minutes.

Had they scored, they would have gone through on away goals and caused a major cup upset. The tie has gone down in UCD folklore, but it's interesting to note that, while Neville remembers the ball striking the bar, he doesn't name the player responsible &, incredible as it may seem in today's digital world, the game wasn't televised & no footage or detailed record of it exists. In 2007, Peter Reid stated that "in the last minute, a lad called Joe Hanrahan had a chance and if he'd have stuck it in, we'd have been out on the away goals rule."

When this was put to the player in question, however, he replied, "If we did hit the bar, I'm fairly certain it wasn't me!" It seems almost certain that it will forever remain a mystery! Whatever the details, Howard Kendall later commented that UCD were the toughest opponents Everton had faced throughout the competition.

Comfortable wins over Inter Bratislava and Fortuna Sittard followed, setting up a semi-final with West German giants Bayern Munich.

Following on from the win over Leicester, Everton consolidated their place at the top of the table by beating West Ham and Stoke City. They were then knocked out of the League Cup at home by Second Division Grimsby Town, having beaten Sheffield United and Manchester United in previous rounds, which was followed by a run of only one win in five league games, the only success being an impressive 5-0 victory over Nottingham Forest.

On December 22nd, a 4-3 defeat at home to Chelsea saw the Toffees replaced at the top of the table by Tottenham.

The Boxing Day fixture saw them beat Sunderland 2-1 at Roker Park and this would be the start of an amazing run of form which would see them take 50 from a possible 54 league points. A 4-0 home win over Newcastle saw Everton go back to the top of the table.

Neville spoke of how the team, despite their outstanding form, tried to stay grounded. Although we were flying high in the league, we didn't think about where it might lead us. We were enjoying our football, enjoying the buzz in the dressing room and on the training ground. Nobody missed training; everybody was in earlier each day & nobody wanted to miss a game. But we tried to keep title thoughts at the back of our minds. "

On the 3rd of April, Everton, who at this point had gone 17 matches without defeat, had a midweek match at White Hart Lane for what was to be a genuine "six pointer" against second-placed Tottenham. There was a lot of media attention in the build up to the fixture, and Everton needed to ensure that there was no repeat of the performance which saw them lose 4-1 in the corresponding fixture on the first day of the season. In the build up to the game, Andy Gray described it as "the most important league game I've played in & probably Everton's most important league game since they clinched the championship in 1970."

A crowd of 48,108 was packed into White Hart Lane for what was being billed as the First Division's match of the season & the Everton side were given a predictably hostile reception as they ran out onto the pitch. It was the Toffees who took the lead after just 10 minutes. A slip up by Tottenham defender Paul Miller let in Andy Gray & his shot from the edge of the box gave the home side's keeper, Ray Clemence, no chance. Glenn Hoddle then shot just wide of Neville's goal before another Spurs error, this time by Mark Bowen, let in Trevor Steven to double the lead. Kevin Sheedy then curled a shot just wide before the

Londoners hit back when Graham Roberts smashed a stunning long-range drive into the top corner.

As Spurs pressed for an equaliser, Neville pulled off a save which, like Gordon Banks' famous stop from Pele in 1970 or the one made by Peter Shilton from Mick Ferguson in 1978, has been shown time and time again. A Tottenham corner was taken short. The resulting cross was met by the head of Mark Falco inside the six-yard box and looked goalbound before Neville somehow got his fingertips to it and turned it over the bar. Even the legendary England goalkeeper, Clemence, stood and applauded his opposite number. Daily Mail reporter, Jeff Powell, wrote, "Southall twisted through the night air like a marlin on the hook to divert the ball over the crossbar." Neville quipped, "I suppose it's a nice way of saying, 'It was right for him!'" He also recalls that Everton captain, Kevin Ratcliffe, yelled at him, "Why didn't you catch it?"

The result made Everton firm favourites for the title and their fine run of form continued. They were confirmed as league champions for the first time since 1970 on May 6th when a crowd of more than 50'000 saw them beat QPR at Goodison Park with five league games still to play. They were to finish the season with 90 points, 13 points ahead of both Liverpool and Tottenham.

Chapter 10
Munich & beyond

As Everton closed in on the 1984/85 League Championship, they'd also reached the semi-finals of both the FA Cup and the European Cup Winners' Cup. First up, on 10th April, they travelled to what was then West Germany to take on Bayern Munich in the first leg of the ECWC semi-final. Bayern almost took the lead when Michael Rummenigge's shot beat Neville, but Kevin Richardson, on for the injured Kevin Sheedy, managed to clear off the line.

Everton and Neville maintained their record of not conceding a goal in the competition and held on for a draw, ensuring their place in the final.

Just three days after their game in Munich, Everton were up against Luton Town in the FA Cup semi-final at Villa Park. The Toffees had progressed to this stage with wins over Leeds United, Doncaster Rovers, and non-league Telford United before being drawn against Ipswich Town at Goodison in the quarter-finals. A Kevin Sheedy free kick had given the home side the lead before a mistake by Neville allowed a Kevin Wilson effort to slip underneath him and find its way into the net.

Ipswich led at the break thanks to Romeo Zondervan's volley. Everton threw everything at the Ipswich goal and, with just 4 minutes remaining, Derek Mountfield steered a Pat van den Hauwe cross past Paul Cooper to take the tie to a replay, where a Graeme Sharp penalty was enough to send Everton through to the semi-final.

At Villa Park, Ricky Hill gave Luton a first-half lead with a strike which left Neville with no chance. After the break, Neville was forced into a fine save as Hill threatened to double both his and Luton's tally for the afternoon. Finally, with only 5 minutes remaining in normal time, Everton equalised when Kevin Sheedy's free kick beat Les Sealey. In extra time, Andy Gray had a shot cleared off the line and Peter Reid was denied from close range by an excellent stop from Sealey. Then, as a replay looked increasingly likely, Mountfield rose above the Luton defence to head home a Sheedy free kick and secure another Wembley date for the Blues.

On April 24th, a crowd of 49,476 was at Goodison Park for the second leg of the semi-final against Bayern Munich. They witnessed what many regard as the greatest game ever played at the famous old venue. The atmosphere both inside and outside the stadium was electric. Neville remembers that it took the team bus 45 minutes to get through the crowds so that they could safely reach the players' entrance. He added, "The crowd never normally affected me in any way, but on this night, they worked as a twelfth man."

During the first half, Trevor Steven, Kevin Sheedy and Graeme Sharp all had chances, but 7 minutes before the break, Bayern took the lead. A drop kick by Neville was picked up by Bayern in their own half & a neat one-two saw Ludwig Kogl bearing down on goal with only Neville left to beat. Neville saved, but the rebound found Dieter Hoeness, who rounded the keeper and slotted the ball home. At half time, Howard Kendall told Neville to keep kicking the ball long and keep the pressure on them. The second half was only 3 minutes old when Everton levelled. A long throw from the right by Gary Stevens was flicked on by Andy Gray and Sharp directed a header into the corner of the net.

Everton threw everything they had at the Gwladys Street End goal. Sharp had a shot saved by keeper Jean-Marie Pfaff, but it was another long throw by Stevens after 73 minutes that led to the Toffees taking the lead. Pfaff failed to gather the ball and it fell to the feet of Gray, who made no mistake from close range. Everton then made sure of victory when Gray set up Trevor Steven, who calmly beat Pfaff from the edge of the penalty area, sending the Goodison crowd wild.

Neville said of the game, "For me it was better than winning the league, better than winning the cup, better than anything that happened before or since." He also told how Gray & Reid had given the Bayern players what he described as "a good kick!" For the Everton supporters, it was a night they would never forget. One story later emerged about a fan who'd attended the match and noticed that the man next to him was wearing carpet slippers.

By half time, his curiosity had got the better of him & he couldn't resist asking the man why, to which he explained that his wife had told him that he couldn't go to the match. There was no way he was going to miss out, so he told her that he was just going to the local shop, where he always went in his slippers. What happened when he finally arrived back home is unknown and probably best left that way!

The European Cup Winners' Cup Final was to be held at Feijenoord Stadium, Rotterdam, on Wednesday 15th May & Everton's opponents were to be Austrian side Rapid Vienna. Rapid had reached the final in controversial circumstances. Trailing 3-0 at Celtic in the 2nd round 2nd leg & therefore 4-3 on aggregate, defender Rudi Weinhofer fell to the floor, claiming to have been struck on the head by a bottle thrown from the crowd. UEFA, at best inept and, at worst, outright corrupt, refused to use the clear evidence provided on film and ordered the game to be replayed. Old Trafford was the neutral venue chosen & the Austrians won 1-0.

Following on from the victory over Bayern Munich in the semi-final, confidence amongst the Everton team was high. Howard Kendall later wrote in his autobiography, Only the Best is Good Enough, that he'd watched Rapid at the earliest opportunity and that they were nowhere near as good as Bayern. Much was made by some of the fact that Neville wore a red shirt that night, not a popular colour with Everton supporters!

He explained that green would have clashed with the Vienna sides' green & white stripes, black with the referee & yellow was only allowed in internationals, leaving him with little to choose from!

Everton moved the ball well in the opening stages, with Kevin Sheedy forcing a save out of Neville's opposite number, Michael Konsel. Paul Bracewell shot just wide before Gray had a goal ruled out for offside. The deadlock was finally broken in the 58th minute when Graeme Sharp pounced on a poor back pass and rounded the keeper before having the presence of mind to look up and find Andy Gray, who volleyed into an empty net.

Trevor Steven then turned superbly in the penalty area, but his shot was brilliantly saved by Konsel. Everton doubled their lead after 73 minutes when a Gary Stevens corner evaded everyone until it reached the unmarked Trevor Stevens, who fired it home from just beyond the far post. Neville was finally called upon to make his first save of note after 82 minutes when he did well to push away a fierce effort by Peter Hrstic. With 85 minutes gone and the Toffees seemingly cruising to victory, Rapid were suddenly back in contention.

The captain and Austrian international, Hans Krankel, who appeared to be offside, took the ball round Neville & halved the deficit. Any thoughts of an Austrian comeback didn't last long, however. Just one minute later, Graeme Sharp sent Kevin Sheedy through to smash the ball high into the Rapid goal.

After the match, there was no time for celebrations as the Everton team flew straight back to Liverpool to prepare for the FA Cup Final against Manchester United, which was scheduled for the following Saturday afternoon. In between, Neville had to travel to London with Howard Kendall to collect the Football Writer's Player of the Year Award.

He became the first goalkeeper to win the prestigious honour since Pat Jennings in 1973, who, at the time of publication, was the last keeper to have won the award. It was proof, if any were required, of how highly regarded he had become. Neville was typically modest about the accolade, saying, "It was nice to get the recognition, but part of me felt a little uneasy about getting all the plaudits when the players in front of me had also done so much." Kendall, however, once remarked, "I am a firm believer that you don't win trophies without an outstanding goalkeeper."

And so to Wembley, with only Manchester United standing between Everton and a historic treble. In the first half, Peter Reid had an effort deflected onto the post by former Toffee defender, John Gidman, before Neville made a comfortable save after Frank Stapleton tried his luck from outside the box.

In the second half, Andy Gray fired a chance wide of the post following excellent work by Reid. With 15 minutes of the 90 remaining, came the incident which the match would be remembered for. Paul McGrath was dispossessed by Reid, who charged forward only to be brought down by United defender Kevin Moran.

Referee Peter Willis ruled it was a professional foul that prevented a goal, and Moran became the first player ever to be sent off in an FA Cup Final. Everton came close in extra time when Bryan Robson headed against his own bar, but the game was decided on 110 minutes when

United's Norman Whiteside curled his shot round van den Hauwe and beyond Neville. A disappointing end to what was, nonetheless, arguably Everton's greatest ever season.

Chapter 11
The ban

While commentating on the 1985 European Cup Winners' Cup Final, Brian Clough said of Everton, "They've got a superb young manager, they've got a magnificent young team and I'm of the opinion that they'll be a force for many years." That was certainly the feeling among the Everton players too. As Neville pointed out, Liverpool had long been considered by many to be the best club side in the world, so when you've just finished the season 13 points ahead of them, who have you got to fear? Not only would the Toffees go into the 1985/86 Division 1 season as defending champions, but they should also have been competing in the European Cup.

Unlike today's Champions League, its predecessor was a knockout tournament & only those finishing as champions of their respective European domestic league took part. However, due to events beyond their control, this talented and confident young Everton side would never get the opportunity to bring the continent's most prestigious trophy to Goodison Park.

Liverpool was scheduled to play Juventus in the European Cup Final on May 25, 1985. The venue was the Heysel Stadium in Brussels. By all accounts, the stadium was in a very poor state of repair and should never have been chosen to stage the match. During the 1980s, English football fans had gained a reputation for violence, especially when travelling abroad. While it was true that a minority of English fans had indeed behaved appallingly and therefore given all their nation's supporters a bad name, the fact that other European countries also had hooligan elements seemed to be ignored.

Trouble flared at the match & as Juventus fans tried to escape, a wall collapsed, leading to the tragic deaths of 39 people. Unbelievably, the game still went ahead, with Juventus winning 1-0.

UEFA, supported by the then British Prime Minister, Margaret Thatcher, proceeded to ban all English clubs from participating in European competition indefinitely. English clubs had dominated European competition for the previous decade, and Neville suggested that, had this not been the case, UEFA may not have been so keen to take this action.

The British government also saw fit to bow down to UEFA rather than stand up for the vast majority of fans who were well behaved. For Everton, who should have been looking forward to taking part in next season's European Cup and whose supporters didn't have a reputation for trouble, the impact of the decision was going to be particularly costly.

During the summer of 1985, Howard Kendall made the surprise decision to sell Andy Gray to Aston Villa. Gray had been a popular player at Goodison and many supporters were outraged by the decision. The player brought in to replace him was Leicester City striker Gary Lineker.
The 1985–86 season began with league champions, Everton, taking on FA Cup winners, Manchester United, in the Charity Shield at Wembley.

Goals from Adrian Heath and Trevor Steven gave Everton a 2-0 win and went some way to avenging the defeat in the FA Cup Final in May. After the match, Neville revealed a t-shirt with the words "I Love My Wife" printed across the front, a reaction to tabloid stories which had surfaced during the summer. When Everton played Sheffield Wednesday, Owls keeper and Neville's former teammate, Martin Hodge, wore a t-shirt proclaiming, "I Love Neville Southall's Wife Too!"

Everton's league title defence began with a run of six games without defeat, which included an excellent 5-1 win over Sheffield Wednesday at Hillsborough. The run came to an end on Queens Park Rangers' Astroturf pitch. Not only did the ball bounce ridiculously on these surfaces, but they were notorious for giving the players friction burns as they slid across the surface. Most goalkeepers would wear tracksuit bottoms, but Neville, never one to conform, would cover himself in Vaseline instead.

On October 12th, Everton were beaten 2-1 by Chelsea at Stamford Bridge and Neville was sent off. In the 19th minute, he was adjudged to have fouled David Speedie inside the box. The referee, Vic Callow, awarded a penalty and then booked Neville for arguing with him. Neville insists, "David Speedie dived over my arm when I was nowhere near him."

In the second half, it got worse when he received a second yellow card for handling the ball outside of the penalty area and therefore had to go. An angry Neville tore off his shirt as he left the field, and Howard Kendall said after the game that he had "let the lads down." In those days, there were no substitute goalkeepers and the captain, Kevin Ratcliffe, was forced to take over in goal. He kept a clean sheet, whereas Neville had conceded 2 goals, something Ratcliffe wasn't going to let him forget in a hurry!

Neville later described how, before the game, he'd felt unusually good. "I was buzzing in the warm-up. I did too much and got sent off. I learned from that. You don't want to burn all your nervous energy if you're feeling good. " In December 1985, Neville signed another contract, this time a six-year deal. It was the longest contract ever offered to anyone by the club.

He acknowledges that he could probably have earned more money by negotiating every couple of years, but he just wanted to play football and couldn't imagine himself playing for anyone other than Everton. He also found himself captaining the side for the first time, albeit in the weakened teams fielded by Howard Kendall for the FA Super Cup. The Super Cup was intended to fill the void left by the European ban but was played in front of largely empty terraces and attracted no sponsorship.

Everton were beaten by Liverpool over two legs in the final. The competition was abandoned after that one season.

In Division 1, Manchester United had gotten off to a terrific start. They had won their first 10 matches and were unbeaten in their first 15, before finally losing at Sheffield Wednesday in November. That was followed, however, by injuries and a dip in form and, although they would stay at the top of the table until February, they eventually finished 4th.

At Everton, Gary Lineker was proving to be a great buy, scoring 31 league goals and 41 in all competitions in his first season with the club. Neville liked Lineker but was amazed at how little he trained. He said that, on the eve of a game, Gary would just sit in the bath! Like Manchester United, Everton had injury problems, losing both Derek Mountfield and Peter Reid for large parts of the season. Despite this, in February, the Toffees had gone 3 points clear at the top of the table following an excellent 2-0 win over Liverpool at Anfield & their chances of retaining the league title were looking good.

However, Neville's season was to be brought to an abrupt end in March. He was playing for Wales against the Republic of Ireland at Lansdowne Road, Dublin. The stadium was also home to the Ireland rugby union team and the Five Nations championships had recently finished, leaving the pitch in terrible condition. In the 66th minute, Neville jumped up for a high ball and as he came down, his foot landed in one of the ruts, dislocating his ankle and tearing the ligaments.

At Everton, Neville's place in goal was taken by Bobby Mimms. Mimms had been signed by Rotherham United during the summer as a replacement for Jim Arnold, who had moved to Port Vale. Despite leading the Division 1 title race for the majority of the last 3 months of the season, Everton would eventually finish as runners-up, 2 points behind Liverpool. They would also lose 3-1 to their neighbours in the FA Cup final.

Many believe that Neville's injury cost Everton the 1985–86 league title, but Neville points out that Mimms only conceded four goals in nine league games and has said that, in his opinion, the outcome would not have been any different.

Chapter 12
The sort of player who wins championships

Following his injury, Neville wasn't what could be described as a "model patient." At the hospital in Dublin, when the doctor told him that he was going to pop the dislocated ankle back into place, the stricken goalkeeper immediately responded by telling him in no uncertain terms that it wasn't going to happen while he was still conscious! Two days later, he returned to Liverpool, having been told that he might not play again until Christmas, which was nine months away.

The club doctor told him not to bother coming into the Bellefield training ground and, instead, recommended that he should take a holiday. However, that was never going to happen & Neville's wife, Eryl, would drive him to Bellefield every day where he immediately worked out a fitness regime which he could manage with one leg in plaster. He acknowledges that his determination to do things his own way and get back on the pitch as soon as possible must have been a nightmare for the club physio, John Clinkard, a man who Neville praises for his incredible patience!

Finally, following months of hard work and rumours that his career was over, Neville, after playing in a couple of reserve fixtures, returned to the first team on October 25th for a game against Watford at Goodison Park. Everton won the match 3-2 and, to his relief, the damaged ankle stood up to the rigours of a tough test without any obvious problems.

It was, however, a difficult season for Neville. He'd found his time on the sidelines mentally challenging and was constantly worried about a re-lapse.

Another new competition, the Full Members Cup, had been created to fill the void left by the European ban, and Everton had reached the quarter-finals where they faced Charlton Athletic at home. With the match finishing 2-2, the tie was decided by a penalty shootout during which a crowd of just over 7,184 witnessed Neville score his only goal for Everton. It was, however, Charlton who would progress to the semi-finals.

One of the effects which the European ban was having on English clubs was that some of the league's best players were being tempted to move abroad to give them the chance to play in the continent's most prestigious competitions.

One such player was Gary Lineker, who left to join Barcelona during the summer. Rather than buying a replacement striker, Kendall bought a centre half, Dave Watson, from Norwich, and a midfielder, Paul Power, from Manchester City. During the early part of the league season, Everton had to deal with injuries to Neville, Derek Mountfield, Paul Bracewell, Pat van den Hauwe, and Gary Stevens. They were unbeaten in their first seven games but then lost three on the trot.

As had been the case two years earlier, however, it was their form during the second half of the season which would clinch the league title for the Blues. During the Christmas period, they won 4-0 at Newcastle and 5-1 at home to Leicester. This was followed by a 3-0 victory over Aston Villa at Goodison Park on New Year's Day and set the tone for the rest of the season.

A five-week period during March and April saw Everton win seven consecutive matches. Neville won man of the match for outstanding performances at both Arsenal and Chelsea when the Toffees won 1-0 and 2-1 respectively. The run was ended by a 3-1 defeat at Anfield, but the title was clinched with two games still left to play, when a Pat van den Hauwe goal was enough to beat Norwich at Carrow Road.

Neville claims that he didn't feel the same elation at winning the championship in 1987 as he had done two years earlier. He'd missed the first part of the season through injury and says that it then took him a couple of months to feel fully fit again.

Overall, he'd found the season difficult with the worry of a recurrence of the injury in the back of his mind. To onlookers, though, he'd been superb, earning praise from sportswriters and opponents alike. After the game at Stamford Bridge, Chelsea striker Kerry Dixon described him as "the sort of player who wins championships." Everton were league champions, but life at Goodison was about to undergo a major change.

Chapter 13
The Harvey years

Everton's success had made Howard Kendall one of the most highly regarded managers in Europe. Coupled with his frustration at not being able to test his side against the continent's finest, it was almost inevitable that he would be tempted by an offer from abroad. As his side closed in on the league championship in the spring of 1987, Kendall had been secretly holding talks with Barcelona with a view to taking over from Terry Venables.

It was, however, another Spanish club, Athletico Bilbao, who, during the summer break, lured Kendall away from Goodison Park.

The man chosen to replace Kendall was Colin Harvey, with former Blues left-back Terry Darracott as his assistant. Harvey had played a huge role in the success that the club had enjoyed over the past three seasons, so, while he felt disappointment at Kendall's decision to leave, Neville thought that at least there would be a certain amount of continuity at the club. Harvey was also an Evertonian through and through and, like Neville, would give his all to bring success to the blue half of Liverpool.

Harvey's reign got off to a good start with another Wembley victory for the Toffees in the Charity Shield, where a Wayne Clarke goal shortly before half time was enough to beat FA Cup winners, Coventry City. During the summer, Neville had surgery on a troublesome knee injury. This meant he missed the Wembley fixture as well as the first few weeks of the season and was again replaced in goal by Bobby Mimms.

In spite of an excellent defensive record in the league that season, which saw them concede just 27 goals in 40 games, Everton never looked like retaining their title. They eventually finished in fourth place, a disappointing 20 points behind first-placed Liverpool. They did, however, beat their neighbours in the League Cup and went on to reach the semi-finals before losing to Arsenal over two legs.

At the end of the season, defender, Gary Stevens, moved north of the border to Rangers &, disappointed with the previous campaign, Harvey brought in West Ham striker, Tony Cottee, for a British record transfer fee of £2 million; Chelsea winger, Pat Nevin; and Bradford City midfielder, Stuart McCall. Neville, however, felt that, despite Harvey's enthusiasm, things were never the same after Kendall's departure & that they missed out on possibly signing players like, for example, Ian Rush when he left Juventus & instead returned to Liverpool.

The 1988/89 season started promisingly with wins over Newcastle and Coventry. However, Everton's form soon faded and they slipped into mid-table, eventually finishing in eighth place with a disappointing 54 points. Neville noticed that, since Kendall's departure, the winning mentality had somehow been lost and that an acceptance of mediocrity had gradually crept into the squad.

They were knocked out of the League Cup in the fourth round by Second Division Bradford City, but fared better in the FA Cup where, after knocking out West Bromwich Albion, Plymouth Argyle, Barnsley and holders Wimbledon, they reached the semi-final and were drawn against Norwich City. In a close and hard-fought game, a Pat Nevin goal gave Everton a 1-0 win and a place in the final.

However, this paled into insignificance with news of the tragic events which were unfolding ninety miles away in Sheffield. In those days, both FA Cup semi-finals were played at the same time on a Saturday afternoon. In the corresponding fixture at Sheffield Wednesday's Hillsborough, Liverpool were playing Nottingham Forest. A crush at the Leppings Lane end of the ground led to the deaths of ninety-seven Liverpool supporters.

When the final whistle was blown at Villa Park, Neville remembers that the Everton players were completely oblivious to the events in South Yorkshire and celebrated reaching the cup final. It was only on the coach home that they found out the enormity of what had happened. Obviously, for the City of Liverpool, the impact was devastating. There was much debate about whether or not the FA Cup should be continued or abandoned for the season. Eventually, the decision was taken to continue &, in the rearranged semi-final which took place at Old Trafford, Liverpool beat Nottingham Forest to set up an all-Merseyside final.

Three weeks before the FA Cup final, Everton had another Wembley date; this time their opponents were Nottingham Forest in the final of the Full Members' Cup, or Simod Cup, as it was known for sponsorship reasons. Tony Cottee put Everton ahead after just eight minutes, holding off both Brian Laws and Des Walker before slotting the ball past Forest goalkeeper Steve Sutton. Gary Parker levelled for Forest, volleying home from a corner. Four minutes after the break, Graeme Sharp restored Everton's lead with an excellent finish, running on to a long pass by Kevin Sheedy and chipping the ball over Sutton.

Neville had to get down quickly to stop an effort from Terry Wilson. Forest again levelled when he finished off a solo run from his own half. Two minutes into extra time, Lee Chapman put Forest ahead for the first time, but nine minutes later, a Cottee header made it 3-3. Sutton then tipped a shot from Cottee onto the bar & then somehow managed to rush back and grab the ball on the line with Sharp rushing in. Three minutes from the end, however, it was Forest who got the winner, with Chapman firing a low cross from Franz Carr into the bottom corner.

The all-Merseyside FA Cup final took place on May 20th, 1989. Neville didn't find it an easy final to play in. He knew that Everton owed it to their fans to try and win the trophy, but there was so much emotion surrounding the match, which made focusing solely on the job in hand very difficult.

Before kick-off, a minute's silence was held in memory of those who had lost their lives & Gerry Marsden, lead singer of Gerry & the Pacemakers, sang the Liverpool anthem, You'll Never Walk Alone. Fittingly, the two sides did their city proud with an entertaining match, with John Aldridge putting Liverpool ahead after just four minutes, with his first-time shot into the top corner giving Neville no chance.

In the second half, Neville had to get down quickly to keep out Peter Beardsley. Liverpool's lead was to last until the last minute of normal time when Stuart McCall forced the ball over the line to put the Toffees level. In extra time, Ian Rush, who had been brought on in place of Aldridge, restored Liverpool's lead before McCall scored his and Everton's second with an excellent strike from outside the box. The day was to belong to the red half of Merseyside, however, with Rush grabbing the winner in what had been a very special and emotional FA Cup final.

The 1989/90 season was an unspectacular one as far as Everton were concerned. Harvey had offloaded many of the players who had brought success to Goodison Park under Howard Kendall, including Paul Bracewell, Trevor Steven, Pat van den Hauwe, Peter Reid and Adrian Heath. The team finished sixth in the league with 59 points, reaching the fifth round of the FA Cup before losing to Oldham Athletic.

They made it to the fourth round of the League Cup, only to lose in controversial circumstances at Nottingham Forest. With just minutes left to play, the referee penalised

Neville for time-wasting by holding on to the ball for too long. Forest were awarded an indirect free kick which Nigel Clough slid across to Lee Chapman, who scored what was the only goal of the game. There was, however, to be more turmoil ahead for Neville during the summer of 1990.

Chapter 14
Three transfer requests & a protest

Since Howard Kendall's departure in 1987, Neville had become increasingly restless at Goodison Park. Much as he liked and respected Colin Harvey, he was unhappy at the team's decline and felt that many of the players who had been brought in were not of the same quality as those who had been allowed to leave. He also felt that, for all his success at the club, he was not shown any respect by many of the directors.

He still loved the club and the fans, but found himself feeling unsettled and put in three separate transfer requests in the space of a year.

Colin Harvey was so concerned about the possibility of losing his first-choice goalkeeper that he started looking for a replacement. He brought Egyptian international goalkeeper, Ahmed Shobier, to Merseyside with a view to signing him. Shobier had impressed with his performances during the 1990 World Cup in Italy.

Problems with obtaining a work permit, however, blocked any chance of a permanent move. There was also a rumour that the Toffees had offered £500'000 for Manchester City's Andy Dibble, but this was denied by Harvey. It is believed that Alex Ferguson was interested in taking Neville to Old Trafford, only to be put off by Everton's £3 million asking price.

The 1990/91 Division 1 season kicked off on August 25th, and it was a day when Neville would find himself the centre of attention for the wrong reasons. Everton were at home to newly promoted Leeds United and, following a less than impressive first half display, found themselves going into the break two goals down. After only a couple of minutes in the dressing room, Neville marched back out onto the pitch and sat down, leaning against a goalpost. The act was seen by many as a protest, but Neville later claimed that, although coming shortly after his transfer request, it could be described as badly timed, he actually just wanted time to think away from the rest of the team. I thought I'd had a shit first half and I just wanted to clear my head, that's all. I've done it before, though I've only ever found one person who remembers it. It was at Plough Lane — the dressing room there was boiling, and they put 52 sugars in the tea!' he said.

Colin Harvey didn't notice Neville leaving the dressing room and only became aware of the incident that evening. He was furious and called Neville at home, fining him two weeks' wages and also suspending him for a fortnight. However, upon realising that his only other goalkeeper was an inexperienced Australian, Jason Kearton, Harvey called again and asked him to come in on Monday for a chat. Two days later, Neville was in the starting line-up for a game at Coventry City.

Chapter 15
Howard's return

Neville wasn't the only member of the Everton side who was unhappy with the team's recent lack of success. There was a split in the dressing room between some of the players who had been there during the successful times and new ones who had joined more recently.

Colin Harvey tried to bring back the team spirit which had been lost, but it backfired spectacularly when, on a night out which he'd organised, a fight broke out between Kevin Sheedy and centre half Martin Keown, leading to unwanted and embarrassing headlines. A run of poor league results followed and finally, after a League Cup defeat at the end of October, Harvey was sacked.

Despite still feeling unsettled at Everton, Neville felt that Harvey should have been given more time to turn the club around. The board had, after all, stood by Howard Kendall when results hadn't been going well & he'd gone on to lead the Toffees to great success. The favourite to replace Harvey was the Oldham Athletic manager and former Everton player, Joe Royle.

What nobody expected, however, was for Kendall to return and immediately re-appoint Harvey as his assistant. Since leaving Bilbao, Kendall had spent almost a year in charge at Manchester City but couldn't resist the offer of returning to the club he loved. Neville was pleased to have the old team of Kendall and Harvey back in charge. He knew their style of management suited him and he didn't have to worry about fitting in with a new type of leadership. The club quickly stabilised under its former boss and they managed to pull away from the relegation zone, eventually finishing in ninth place.

In 1991, Everton reached the final of the Full Members' Cup for the second time in three seasons. The sponsorship of the competition had changed and it was now known as the Zenith Data Systems Cup. In a physical encounter, Everton were beaten 4-1 after extra time by Crystal Palace, with Polish winger Robert Warzycha scoring the Toffees' only goal. After the game, Neville, unhappy at the performance, refused to go up to the Royal Box to collect his medal.

In the summer of 1991, Graeme Sharp left Everton for Oldham Athletic. Sheedy & Ratcliffe were to follow Sharp out of the door, leaving Neville as the only member of the 1985 championship winning side who was still at the club. Peter Beardsley was brought in from Liverpool along with Rangers striker Mo Johnston. However, despite Kendall's efforts to rebuild, the Goodison faithful endured their worst season for a decade, finishing 12th in the league with 53 points from their 42 games, although they did beat league champions, Arsenal, 3-1 in their first home match of the campaign.

Kendall became increasingly frustrated at the lack of team spirit that had been so evident during the glory days of the mid-eighties.

1992/93 was the season in which the old Football League Division 1 was replaced by the FA Premier League. Money mattered more in football than ever before, and it was rumoured that Everton were struggling financially and that Martin Keown was sold to Arsenal in early 1993 to pay off debts.

They continued to underachieve, finishing thirteenth on 53 points, just four points ahead of relegated Crystal Palace. Despite this, Neville was happy with his own form and felt more settled at the club than he had for some time. For Howard Kendall, though, life wasn't easy. He was trying to turn the situation on the pitch around when there was no money to spend on new players. Late in 1993, he wanted to sign Dion Dublin from Manchester United, but the Everton board refused to sanction the transfer, prompting Kendall to resign as manager.

As reserve team coach, Jimmy Gabriel took over as interim manager until a successor to Howard Kendall was found. Under Gabriel's leadership, they lost six out of seven matches. Former England manager Bobby Robson was a favourite to take over at Goodison, but he chose to stay in Portugal, managing FC Porto.

Instead, the Everton board went for Norwich City manager Mike Walker. He brought with him the assistant manager, David Williams, meaning there was no longer a place for Colin Harvey at the club. Everton's pattern of play was changed by Walker and Williams, but it wasn't a success and, on the last day of the season, Everton found themselves in the relegation zone. The Toffees were at home to Wimbledon and had to get a better result than Sheffield United, who were away to Chelsea. Even a win wouldn't be enough for Everton if the Blades won at Stamford Bridge.

Wimbledon went ahead at Goodison Park through a Dean Holdsworth penalty, which Neville got a hand to but couldn't keep it out. The Dons then doubled their lead after 20 minutes when Gary Ablett couldn't stop a shot from Andy Clarke from crossing the line following a mix up in the Blues defence. Shortly before the break, Everton were awarded a penalty when Anders Limpar went down in the box.

Nobody seemed too keen on shouldering the responsibility, so Neville volunteered to take the kick himself, before Graham Stuart took the ball and made no mistake from the spot. Holdsworth missed a couple of good chances for Wimbledon before a superb long-range shot from Barry Horne put Everton level. With ten minutes to play, Stuart got his second to win the game for Everton and keep them in the Premier League. Sheffield United lost 3-2 at Chelsea and were relegated.

Chapter 16
Royle appointment

In spite of the win on the final day of the 1993/94 season, which kept Everton in the top-flight, all was not well in the Goodison Park dressing room. Mike Walker's training methods and style of play were not popular amongst the players and some were becoming openly hostile towards the manager. The fans weren't happy either, and Neville found himself on the end of abuse from a minority of them.

He even received a threat to kill his family, which he believes that the club didn't take seriously. The start to the season was the worst in Everton's history, failing to win any of their first twelve league matches.

In November, after just ten months in charge, Walker was sacked. His replacement was former Everton player, Joe Royle, who had been in charge at Oldham for over twelve years and had guided them into the top-flight. Royle changed the way the team played to a quicker, more direct style and, gradually, performances improved, with the club finishing in 15th place. Along the way, they went on a club record run of seven consecutive clean sheets.

The new manager's first game in charge was a 2-0 home win over Liverpool. It was Neville's 35th appearance in a Merseyside derby, breaking Bruce Grobbelaar's record. Neville still holds the record, having played in a total of 41. Royle's first season in charge also saw silverware return to Goodison Park. In the FA Cup, Everton had beaten Derby County, Bristol City, Norwich and Newcastle, before an impressive 4-1 win over Tottenham in the semi-final. In the final, as was the case ten years earlier, they faced Manchester United.

In the final, Everton went in front when Paul Rideout headed past Peter Schmeichel after Graham Stuart's shot had rebounded off the crossbar. And Neville pulled off an incredible double save from Paul Scholes, as well as denying both Gary Pallister and Nicky Butt, and a season which had started so badly for Everton had ended with a major trophy.

As usual, Neville didn't stay around for the victory celebrations, choosing instead to drive home. On his way back, he stopped to help some Manchester United supporters whose car had broken down, driving them to the nearest garage. Neville jokingly says that he debated whether or not he should stop before deciding, "Yeah, we beat them and won the cup!"

Before the start of the 1995/96 season, Everton held a testimonial for Neville, which included a match against Celtic at Goodison Park. It was also at this time that he received his MBE from the Queen. The season itself began with another Wembley appearance, this time against Premier League champions, Blackburn Rovers, in the Charity Shield, with a goal from Vinny Samways ensuring that the Toffees got off to a winning start.

Everton's form continued to improve under Joe Royle and they would eventually finish in sixth place, just short of qualifying for the UEFA Cup. Their hopes of retaining the FA Cup, however, were ended when they were beaten by third-tier Port Vale.

Neville felt that, at the age of 36, he had played well throughout the season. He hadn't missed any of the clubs' 49 competitive matches. It was, however, no secret that Joe Royle was looking for his successor. During the summer, he signed Paul Gerrard, who had been Royle's first choice goalkeeper at Oldham. He also tried to sign Nigel Martyn from Crystal Palace & the deal looked to be done before Howard Wilkinson persuaded him to join Leeds instead, much to Royle's disgust.

Wolves contacted Everton to enquire about signing Neville and Royle, but Everton seemed keen on selling. Neville went to meet Wolves manager, Mark McGhee, and watch a pre-season friendly. He says Wolves, he says, offered to double his Everton salary, but when he got back to Merseyside, Royle's attitude had changed and he said he'd match what Wolves had offered to him. Neville agreed to sign a new two-year contract.

Chapter 17
The Leaving of Everton

The 1996/97 season had started reasonably well for Everton, with a win at home to Newcastle on the opening day followed by draws at Manchester United and Tottenham. They then endured a run of poor results which included a 4-0 defeat at Wimbledon and were knocked out of the League Cup, beaten over two legs by York City of the third tier.

This was followed by some indifferent form but, over the busy Christmas period, they really began to struggle, with defeats against Middlesbrough, Wimbledon and Blackburn. In the FA Cup, having seen off Swindon Town in the third round, the Toffees were drawn at home to Bradford City, who, at that time, were in what is now the Championship. Bradford won the tie 3-2 and although Neville felt that he wasn't at fault for any of the goals, Joe Royle responded by dropping him from the team, replacing him with Paul Gerrard.

Neville didn't feel that Joe Royle had given him an adequate explanation for leaving him out of the side and believed that he was simply made a scapegoat for the team's poor performances. An injury to Gerrard saw Neville briefly back in the first team, but it was now obvious that he was Royle's second choice.

As the March transfer deadline approached, it was looking like he would be signed by Chelsea, but Royle blocked the move because he didn't have a replacement goalkeeper. Although Neville didn't want to leave Everton, he wanted to play first team football and if that meant moving to another club, so be it. He argued with Royle, but the manager wouldn't change his mind. The following day, after a disagreement with the Everton board over attempts to sign Tore Andre Flo from the Norwegian club, Brann, Joe Royle resigned.

Captain, Dave Watson, was made caretaker manager for the remainder of the season. A story has since done the rounds on Merseyside about how close Neville actually came to getting the job. Apparently, the morning after Royle's departure, head of communications, Alan Myers, was in the Bellefield training ground car park with the chairman, Peter Johnson.

They were discussing who should take over the role until Royle's successor was appointed. Johnson told Myers, "I have a shortlist of two: Dave Watson and Neville Southall, but I'm leaning towards Neville." At this point, Neville pulled up, got out of his car, and shouted, "Alright Alan, you fat c***!" Johnson turned to Myers and said, "I think the shortlist is down to one!" With Watson in charge, Neville was reinstated as first team goalkeeper and the Toffees finished the season in 15th place with just forty-two points, two points ahead of relegated Sunderland.

During the summer break, the search for Royle's permanent replacement began. Bobby Robson again turned the job down, as did former striker Andy Gray. Eventually, with the new season approaching and under increasing pressure from the supporters, Johnson appointed Howard Kendall, who until recently had been in charge at Sheffield United, for his third spell as Everton manager, with Adrian Heath as his assistant.

Kendall's latest reign at Everton didn't get off to the best of starts. They won just once in their first five games, the only success being a 2-1 home win over West Ham. On the 16th of September, they were away to Scunthorpe United in the League Cup. Howard left Neville out of the team, putting Paul Gerrard in goal. The next league match was at home to Barnsley, and Neville was expecting to be recalled. Kendall, however, kept Gerrard in the side until a

League Cup third round tie at Coventry, when the former Oldham keeper had a nightmare and Everton lost 4-1. Just three days later, Liverpool were the visitors to Goodison Park and Neville found himself back in the starting line-up. A Neil Ruddock own goal and a superb solo effort from teenager Danny Cadamateri gave the blue half of Merseyside the bragging rights.

It was, however, to be followed by a run of eight winless games, the sixth of which, a 2-0 defeat at home to Tottenham, not only left Everton at the bottom of the Premier League but also turned out to be Neville's last appearance for the club.

Howard Kendall signed goalkeeper Thomas Myhre from Viking of Norway for £800,000 in November. Myhre had played twenty-seven times for the Norwegian Under-21 side and was regarded as a keeper with a bright future. On December 6th, Everton were away to Leeds United in the Premier League and Neville was fully expecting to play. On the morning of the match, however, Kendall's goalkeeping coach, Mervyn Day, told him that Kendall wanted to see him in his hotel room. After much thought, Kendall told him that he'd decided to drop him from the team and put Myhre in goal instead.

As Neville walked back to his own room, he bumped into Day, who had been completely unaware of Kendall's decision and found it difficult to understand.

Myhre played well in a goalless draw at Leeds, and on the Monday morning, Kendall approached Neville and told him bluntly that he was to stay away from Goodison Park and the Bellefield training ground. That was it, after sixteen years at the club which he loved. He was finished as an Everton player. Neville tells us how he then asked for a transfer so that he could carry on his playing career, only for Kendall to offer him a coaching role. When he turned that down, Kendall told him simply to go and find another club. Neville would later say that he could see that Neville was losing some of his agility, and telling him that he was effectively finished at Everton was one of the most difficult things he had to do.

In his time at Everton, Neville played a club record 751 times for the first team, including 578 league appearances. He won the European Cup Winners' Cup, both the league championship and FA Cup twice, and the Charity Shield on three occasions. He has achieved legendary status at Goodison Park and is regarded by many as Everton's greatest ever player.

Chapter 18
Life after Goodison

Despite being told to stay away from the club, Neville continued to train alone at Everton's Bellefield training ground. He wanted to stay busy, but also realised that by staying match fit he had a better chance of finding another club. He also thought that the more he annoyed Howard Kendall, the more likely he was to help him move on! Sure enough, in December 1997, he was called into Kendall's office and told that the Southend United manager, former West Ham and England centre half Alvin Martin, wanted to speak to him. Neville agreed to join The Shrimpers on loan & made a total of nine appearances for the Second Division side.

When his loan spell at Roots Hall came to an end, Neville was back to training alone until his agent put him in touch with Stoke City. They were managed by Chris Kamara, who Neville took an instant liking to and accepted his offer. Stoke, however, were struggling in the First Division (what is now the Championship) and the atmosphere at the club was described as toxic. Neville had only been there for two months when, under pressure from the board and fans, Kamara resigned.

At the time, he was struggling to deal with the death of his father, and Neville described the lack of empathy shown by the Stoke City board as "one of the most disgraceful things I've ever witnessed in football." Neville's former manager, Alan Durban, who was at that time coaching the youth team, was put in temporary charge but was clearly no fan of Neville, and infuriated him by telling him, "I'll let you manage the reserves.

So long as you keep your head down and do whatever I tell you, I won't tell everybody you're a bad influence. " Durban was unable to stop the rot and Stoke were relegated. After the match, Neville walked out of the Britannia Stadium and never returned, later saying, "One of the worst episodes of my life had drawn to a close." The next stop was Doncaster Rovers, who were managed by Neville's former Everton team-mate Ian Snodin. Rovers had been relegated from the Football League, meaning Neville was back in non-league football for the first time since he left Winsford United. His short-term deal was brought to an abrupt end by a hamstring injury sustained in a game against Southport.

Following his recovery, Neville found himself without a club until, at the age of forty and unsure whether he would play again, Torquay United manager, Wes Saunders, called him and asked him to sign for the Devon side. At first, Neville wasn't too keen on the idea, given how far away Torquay was from his North Wales home. However, Alex Watson, brother of Neville's former Everton team-mate Dave, played for the club & it was Dave who persuaded Neville that he should sign.

Neville played his first game for Torquay against Hull City on December 12th, 1998. He found facilities there much more basic than at Everton. Torquay trained in what the players dubbed "Dogshit Park," which was a particularly unpleasant place when you were a goalkeeper! In his book, Inside The Gulls, Dave Thomas tells how physio Norman Medhurst couldn't find a shirt big enough for Neville and took a pair of scissors to the biggest one he had! Neville made 27 appearances that season for the Gulls and was voted Player of the Year.

In all, he played 61 times for Torquay before leaving by "mutual consent." He said that it was the happiest he'd been since he'd left Everton & said that he didn't want to leave Plainmoor. He did, however, state that, "Although I told Wes, 'I'm not interested in your job,' I think as time went on, he found it difficult to have me there." He went on to say, "Considering that I only planned to stay for a few weeks, I absolutely loved my time at Torquay. It was the closest I ever got to Everton in how I felt about a club. I still follow them all these years later.

Shortly after leaving Torquay, Neville was approached by Bradford City manager, Paul Jewell. Bradford had been promoted to the Premier League and Jewell was looking for a goalkeeping coach, a role which Neville accepted. There were already three senior goalkeepers at Valley Parade, but within weeks of Neville's joining, all three were injured, leaving Jewell with a choice between an untried teenager or his forty-one-year-old coach.

Neville got the nod and found himself back in Premier League action for a local derby against Leeds United. Leeds won the match 2-1 and Neville found himself coming in for criticism from the media. He hadn't trained much since leaving Torquay and was accused of being too fat for the Premier League.

Bradford avoided relegation on the last day of the 1999/2000 season, but Paul Jewell left the club to take over at Sheffield Wednesday. Jewell was replaced by assistant manager Chris Hutchings, who retained Neville as goalkeeping coach. Hutchings, however, was sacked after just twenty-one games in charge. Heart of Midlothian manager, Jim Jeffries, was brought in to fight the relegation battle which Bradford found themselves in.

Jeffries and Neville had differences of opinion, most notably with Neville insisting that Matt Clarke was the best keeper at the club. Jeffries, however, sent Clarke to Bolton on loan. Bradford were relegated at the end of the season and Neville left Valley Parade.

At the start of the 2001/02 season, Neville played three games in the Welsh League for Rhyl before joining up with his former Everton captain, Kevin Ratcliffe, at Shrewsbury

Town. Ratcliffe was the manager of The Shrews, and he needed him to fill in for first-choice keeper Ian Dunbavin. In December 2001, Neville accepted an offer to manage a struggling Conference side, Dover Athletic. His assistant was Clive Walker, who had previously had two spells as manager of Northampton Town. However, Neville found the set-up at Dover far from ideal and was sacked following a club takeover, with Walker taking over as manager.

Shortly before Christmas 2004, Neville took over as manager of Hastings United. He spent a year there on a part-time basis, although he insisted that the job required a full-time commitment, before a disagreement with the chairman led to him leaving the club. Other than a brief spell as caretaker manager at Margate in 2009, it was to be Neville's last job in football.

Chapter 19
Neville on...

Referees.

"Good teams always get more decisions. That's partly why they're good teams. Whether it's because they're cleverer players, I don't know, but you get more decisions in your favour if you're at the top. "

Media.

I was told by the lads (Everton team-mates) to talk to The Sun one year & was told that I had to ask for payment at the end, which I did, thinking that's the way it was done. The paper published details of my request and made me look like an absolute twat. "

Tickets for the 1984 FA Cup Final

"Everybody was desperate for a ticket. My family must have grown by about 300 because, all of a sudden, aunties who I'd never heard of started to emerge.

Everton did not follow Liverpool and banned The Sun for its reporting of the Hillsborough disaster.

Show some class and courage by outlawing The Sun.

The frugality of FAW in the 1980s

By the time they took your room service bill off, your match fee, your phone calls, and tickets for friends and family, you didn't have any money. I don't think I earned a penny from Wales. In fact, I probably owed them money in the end. "

Using a hostile crowd to his advantage.

I could walk up to, say, the Stretford End & pretend to examine the pitch & they'd all go, 'fuck off you twat' & throw stuff at you. I'd go in & think, 'I can use that now.' And if you win, at the end of the game you can just go, "'bye' & they all go bananas."

Interviews immediately after a game.

They ask, "How do you feel?" What do they expect them to say-I feel absolutely shit to be fair? I think it's really intrusive. I think there should be no interviews on the pitch and no interviews with the manager until two hours after the game. "

Managers stay connected with the fans.

"The manager should have somebody in the stand who listens to what people say around them because a lot of the time they get it so wrong. They say, "We played well," when everybody in the stands says, "We played shit," so they lose their credibility with the crowd. I think they need to take the crowd's point of view into the press conference. "

threatened with arrest when someone complained about him swearing.

"They're going to arrest 10,000 people behind the goal, are they if I make a complaint?"

recording of Everton's 1985 FA Cup final song, Here We Go.

"I never went. Singing's not my thing, to be fair. And when they went on with Terry Wogan, a few of them were pissed anyway. I didn't like that side of it. It's a nice side if you want to do it, but you should be doing your job. "

Being asked by Caroline if he was thinking about a singing career

"Err, no."

Howard Kendall's acceptance of his individuality.

"Everything I did was to make me better, which would then make the team better. He trusted me and I trusted him. I think that's the best way to do things. "Trust is better than forcing things on you.

Alan Partridge

"I don't like Alan Partridge because he managed me under the name of Mike Walker."

In comparison to my squandered youth.

"You stood behind goals & I stood in front of them. It's not that different. "

On the drive home after a match

"If I'd made a mistake, I wanted to run somebody over, but by the time I was home, I'd started to settle."

Chapter 20
Making the world a better place

Neville has been offering his social media followers one of Teesside's most popular charities. He has always used his power to help people, and in this case, he offered to hand over his social media account in order to make the world a better place. He even authorized people to use his social media as a place of discussion about various problems.

You might know Nev from his Twitter presence. And if you don't, you should get familiar with @NevilleSouthall.

Nev's Twitter output is usually a mix of blandly remembered back-in-my-day platitudes and often-questionable and morally dubious banter. Given that the demographic of their followers is predominantly an entity of 'football fans', they'd be letting themselves in for gruelling afternoons spent receiving furious replies and being told to "stick to the football, mate." Typical Nev just doesn't give a fuck.

The same is true of the vast majority of celebrity tweeters. They might have an interest in the issues, but this rarely extends beyond self-aggrandising 'philanthropy'—usually amounting to turning up at lavish charity galas, retweeting TED talks, and occasionally opining that peace and love are nice. @NevilleSouthall is different. Very different.

I first became aware of Nev's online presence several years ago. He is one of the few celebrities of any renown espousing with vocal support for Jeremy Corbyn's Labour. Nev would doggedly post about the evils of austerity and cuts to public services, urging critical-support until the wee hours.

A particular highlight: the development of his own homegrown high-grade meme about skeletons. Having idly mused on repurposing the bones of the dead for civic duties - as street-signs, and lampposts. Nev converted his obsession into a means to attack Tory policy.

> **"2 skeletons talking one said to other won't be long before we get our pension Mays Britain"**

The remarkable thing about Nev's skeleton tweets is that every single one is funny. The bit hasn't worn off. His attitude to spelling, grammar, and the correct use of paragraph breaks gives the tweets an impeccable rhythm and delivery that infinite comedy writers on infinite contrived 'Weird Twitter' accounts couldn't replicate. And that's not to say they're unintentionally funny—each new punchline consistently outdoes the last. Nev knows exactly what he's doing.

An aspect of his account that elevates it to "must-follow" status: it's just so wholesome. He dedicates an enormous amount of time to making his small corner of the internet a truly affirming presence. If there's a rescue dog in need of a home, Nev seeks it out and gives it a retweet.

If there's a follower raising money for a worthy cause—from homelessness to food banks, to health complications—he gives it the full weight of his support. If someone has sent him something, he makes sure to reply regardless of who they are, and with a gentleness that can't help but warm your heart. It's almost worrying to wonder how much of his free time is spent performing these tiny acts of internet kindness, but it's a rare and uplifting thing that he does. He's just an honest and earnestly nice guy.

Nev doesn't disappoint. He found himself mentoring children from disadvantaged backgrounds who had left (or been forced out of) education. His time with these kids, and his desire to help those with unrealised potential, resulted in Southall working in special-needs schools across the country and starting a consultancy that aimed to help unemployed young people outside the education system.

This experience was fraught with frustration. These services were essential, but the government didn't agree. Austerity measures imposed by then-Education Secretary Michael Gove resulted in sweeping cuts to-and in some cases, the complete removal of funding for these schemes. Nev worked in schools in west Wales, attempting to find children work and seeking investment from businesses.

Outside of this, he would regularly be involved in-whether by simply promoting his attendance or by speaking at-activist rallies and charity events. For all the exaltation of his tweets, his commitment extends beyond his @.

He's carried that same hunger for self-improvement beyond his playing days. Finding himself less versed in gender and trans-rights issues and terms than he'd like, Southall sought out the knowledge of activists, writers, and campaigners, as well as asking members of the trans community if they'd be willing to share their experiences with him.

Southall's endeavours to rectify his ignorance set him streets ahead of his peers.

The manner in which Southall went about his willingness to listen connected with me and took me back to why I first contacted him. I think I have Neville's same appetite for curiosity. I read about these things. I am one of these people. I have experienced most of the things that Nev is passionate about. That's not really the point though, is it? Managing to prevent yourself being insensitive as self-protectionism isn't the same as a sincere effort to understand and empathise with an experience.

As Nev shows, people aren't trying to catch you out, and they are more than happy to help if you demonstrate a good-faith readiness to learn. Finally, the Nev tweets which gave me the most pause for reflection were this series, expressing a sentiment simply, yet strangely beautifully:

"I was hoping that people would come on a certain day of the week to talk. What I envisioned was that every single day, there'd be somebody on my Twitter, not me. So I got to do a Monday and a Friday, and I was hoping to have trans people, but I think they found it too much as well.

Really? "Nev explained as we discussed the Twitter takeover. I was interested in helping Nev with that and being part of the takeover.

"I like Twitter because it brings me into contact with people I'd never meet," Southall says. "I like what makes people tick. So I'm thinking: 'How mentally strong have these women got to be in the sex industry?' Even if you like it, at some stage you're going to get hurt."

If many people become parochial and dogmatic as they grow older, then Southall is on a quest to open himself up and learn. Before he allowed his Twitter page to become an occasional platform for sex workers, Southall admitted his preconceptions. "I thought it was just people stuck on street corners." But when you talk to them, they become real. If you cut them, they bleed. If you tell them a joke, they will sometimes laugh. They hurt, they cry. Eventually, they die the same as you and me. We think of them as statistics or problems, but they can come from your family or friends.

When they first came on my Twitter, I wasn't sure how they'd be taken. But people listened because they were genuinely interested. How often do you get a chance to listen to a sex worker or ask them questions? People are engaged positively and sensibly. I've got a bit of flak because if I speak up for sex workers, some people think I'm supporting the trafficking of women. That's stupid.

It could be your mum, your daughter, your sister, or your brother. You don't know who is doing sex work. I'm trying to get across what they actually do and the barriers they face. "

Southall adopts a similarly inclusive approach when working with people on drug awareness, the LGBT community, and "this week we have a big mental health push, a BAME evening, the police are coming on and people who address knife crime".

The subject that had the biggest impact was the LGBT one. Nev got 30,000 new followers within a week. More importantly, he was learning new stuff. "I started with the LGBT stuff because if the kids at school asked a question, I wouldn't have a clue." But I spoke to a few trans people about operations. They were really nice and explained stuff I knew nothing about.

It's all about uniting people. If we could unite all sex workers, that would change their lives for ever. The government would have to listen to them. If you unite all LGBT people, there are millions. If you do the same with the mental health people and all the charities came together, it would be powerful. "

Nev gets followed by many politicians and admits that he has blocked a few. "I've also blocked people from the Sun."

The furore over Raheem Sterling and calls for England to drop him because of a still-incomplete tattoo of a gun on his leg – which the Manchester City forward chose to have done in memory of his father, who was shot dead when he was two years old. "That was brought up by some prick," Southall recalls. Piers Morgan is a prick. What gives him the right to say what can be on your body? If Sterling had tattooed a massive cock on his leg, I would say: 'It reminds me of Piers Morgan.' "

There appears to be a racial undertow in the tabloids' hounding of Sterling, but Southall believes "he gets abused because he's got lots of cash". He says: "Anybody successful in this country gets tonnes of abuse." Harry Kane? The best thing since sliced bread. I bet at the World Cup he gets called a hopeless wanker. The Sun will be following all of those footballers around, hoping they fuck up. Why do we love Frank Bruno? We love people who allow us to say: "Oh, he's a great loser." Fuck off.

I was glad Kane said, 'We should talk about winning it'— because they can. "

Is Southall looking forward to the World Cup? "I am – but it's in the wrong country." Why would you go to a country where human rights are shit? Where homophobia is horrendous. England should have sent the LGBT team to represent them. Fuck Putin. Here's our gay team. What are you going to do now?' Or they should send an all-black team, just to annoy Putin. "

Chapter 21
Build a rapport, treat them like adults

Neville stumbled into a community scheme which took on young people from dysfunctional or difficult backgrounds in Dover who had fallen out of mainstream education and, using football training as an incentive, got them into work. "No big deal, no massive initiative," Southall reflects, with the same modesty he is remembered for at Everton.

There were seven of them, all with their own battles and struggles, and Nev was just trying to find a way to get through to them.

"I found that what had worked in the dressing room worked with them. Don't get offended or hold grudges. You take the p***, build a rapport, treat them like adults, don't preach. When there's mutual respect, the learning takes care of itself. "

It's fair to say that the austerity policies of the coalition and Conservative governments did not make Southall's new path through what are known as NEETs (young people 'not in education, employment or training') a terribly easy one. He studied for an education qualification in Canterbury while managing Hastings United, an hour and a half's drive away, yet repeatedly found funding cuts and a need to start again. But the jolts sent him into new places beyond the gilded world of football.

He worked with asylum seekers in Dover, teaching them football coaching concepts which they took into schools. 'Incredibly polite kids and very good.' He worked with young people whose struggle with basic maths was no fault of their own. One teenager could understand 7 x 2 but could not get his head around 2 x 7 and found that soul-destroying until Southall brought a dartboard in, spent a morning throwing darts at it with him, and suddenly the mist lifted.

In 2014, Southall started working as a teaching assistant at Canolfan Yr Afon. Canolfan yr Afon was a pupil referral unit (PRU) maintained by Blaenau Gwent local authority. It provided education for up to 38 pupils at key stages 3 and 4, who had social, emotional, and behavioural difficulties. In addition, places were available at all key stages for pupils who required individual or group tuition. Staff from Canolfan yr Afon supported these placements.

Unfortunately, the school closed on December 31st, 2017. 14 pupils were accessing community or home tuition. Many of the pupils were also registered at local mainstream schools. All pupils had special educational needs (SEN) and nine pupils had statements of SEN.

There were six girls at the PRU. Very few pupils were from minority ethnic backgrounds. Most pupils came from homes where English was the predominant language.

Approximately half of all pupils are entitled to free school meals. Very few of the pupils were looked after by the local authority. The key stage 4 provision offered GCSE, entry level and vocational qualifications.

Where appropriate, the PRU made provision for older pupils to attend college placements. Neville worked at the school for three days a week where he helped to prepare pupils for the world of work, including with their interview techniques, CV writing, identifying skills, and how to dress and behave at work. He also helped the school in its goal to give sport and physical activity a higher profile in youngsters' lives.

As someone who was told he would never make it in life, Neville said: "If I can help to turn just one of these pupils' lives around and find them a successful work placement, maybe even leading to a permanent job, then it would be a success."

"Growing up, I was always told by my teachers that I was rubbish and that I would never make it, and yet I went on to have the football career that I did. All that young people need is for someone to believe in them and support them.

" I am going to be working with the pupils and the local business community to try to break down barriers and set up some placements. Sport is a big part of this work as it helps to build confidence, trust and tolerance and develops social skills and teamwork.

Neville carried out similar work with pupils in London and wanted to carry on this work in his home country.

Ian Roberts, headteacher at Canolfan Yr Afon, said: "It's absolutely fantastic to have Neville on board. He is a natural with the young people and he is someone that they can really look up to and respect. Neville is someone who's just 'got it' when it comes to working with our pupils. "

"We are currently finding it difficult to find work placements for our young people for a variety of reasons, and we are hoping that the work Neville is doing will turn this around."

"We recently had one of our young people find a full-time job after being accepted by a local hair salon on work experience – this is one success story; we hope there are many more to come."

Good features of the PRU's work include:
- A reduction in the level of exclusions;
- The caring relationships that teaching assistants establish with pupils

- The increase in vocational curriculum opportunities for older pupils and
- The appropriate progress that the PRU made in implementing the national literacy and numeracy framework.

I worry it seems patronising to praise this legend but I feel there's something more than that with Nev, something genuinely quite affecting and inspiring.

Chapter 22
I'm basically a nugget

"Allen runs it at the moment because I'm coming off it for a bit. I occasionally go back on it and do stuff. The idea was to do something because we got a podcast and tried to link the Twitter takeover to the podcast. So, if we have somebody on that I'm talking to about racism, like a Twitter takeover, then onto the podcast.

So we're trying to make the podcast into the sort of thing that we do on Twitter, because when people normally do a podcast, and I've done a few, it's to talk about their careers and all that sort of stuff, and I think I want the extension of that. You can hear the people talk and see them and we can ask the questions and stuff. " Nev explained when asked about the 90 minutes with Nev podcast.

"I'm trying to get support for suicidal people. I'm going to have sex workers on one show, but they're always busy, which is a good sign, I suppose. The idea is that we do exactly the same thing and we're not going to try and be a podcast when we get big stars on and talk about all sorts of shit. It's just basically, I want an extension of what we're doing. " he continued.

"I work on a basis. I'm basically a nugget, so if I bring people on the show, then they've got to tell the story and they've got to tell what they're interested in. If I were to talk to you, is it about being a lesbian? I wouldn't have a fucking clue. But you could tell me, because that is what you are. " Nev discussed whilst making reference to my sexuality. He didn't do this with any intent, but to make a point that he didn't have a clue about homosexuality, but I did.

"It's good for the real people to be there. I've got some other stuff, and I think what about the practicalities? I think that interests me more. I like history. Everyone talks about the battles, right? But nobody ever says, well, it took this long to get here and we had to do this."

Nev talked about the important things that really matter to people, like who they are and the people around them. "When you grow up in this day and age, they see so much stuff by the time they are 12, 14 years of age, but there's so much more that's accepted by them than people my age."

I tell Nev how I've been fortunate enough with my family, having five children. I've been fortunate enough that I've been able to talk to the older children about different aspects, such as my relationship with my wife and that I am bisexual and stuff. I think it's a certain generation that's a problem.

> "I think we get so fucking hung up in this country. Everything's got to be a crisis. Everybody has to make issues out of everything.

It's probably the wrong thing to say to you, but you don't sell tickets and make people come and watch you in bed with your wife. Nobody's forced anybody into it. Why does it bother other people? I never quite got why it bothers other people, but we have a society where it seems to matter what other people are thinking. Nobody knows you apart from you, because nobody knows you, do they? "

I'm not quite sure if Nev was having a rant or just extremely passionate about the subject.

Chapter 23
I think we fight too much to feel good

I first contacted Nev via Twitter. I was campaigning to introduce quarterly (every 3 months) mental health check-ups for men with their GP's, which could prevent the type of situations that affected Gary Speed, Darren Eadie, Dean Windass, and Paul Gascoigne—(who also believes that all football clubs should have their own in-house counsellor.) I had written a report which I sent to the FA on the mental health of players, but I was ignored both by the FA and the PFA.

I explained to Neville how 102 professional footballers had taken their own lives. Through my research, I found that the average age of a footballer taking their own life in the UK was 37. Many of the players are nearing or have reached the end of their careers at this age.

I described to Neville how I believed professional players needed better support when they were approaching the end of their career. Those involved in football at all levels need to understand the importance of mental health and what mental health is. Mental health issues can be harder to spot than physical injuries, but how much support the sufferer receives can make a big difference to their recovery.

I told Nev how the organisation I founded-Football Awareness of Mental Health (FAMH) had researched in great depth and found that 100 male footballers and 2 female footballers had taken their own lives dating back as far as 1908 and yet it is still happening today. It was with these statistics that I was campaigning for all GP surgeries to invite male patients to quarterly (every 3 months) mental health check-ups just like they would with physical checks... FAMH believes that having these regular check-ups not only opens up opportunities for men to speak out, but could possibly prevent a mental illness turning into a suicide.

Nev agreed with the work that I was doing and suggested I contact Dr. Sharon McDonnell, the Director of Suicide Bereavement UK, Honorary Research Fellow at the University of Manchester and a specialist in suicide bereavement research, training and consultancy. He also suggested contacting Tom Chapman, a public speaker and founder of The Lions Barbers, which is an original multi-award-winning barbers creating a safe place for men to talk to someone they trust. "Why don't you do a take over of my account to raise awareness of your work?" You never know who looks at it, "Nev said.

It was amazing for Nev to suggest it. "Are you sure?" I asked. "You know your subject, so why not?" he replied. "God bless you, I've just had a reply from 'the Secret drug addict so I'll crack on with that" I explained.

After wishing me good luck and said how the Secret Drug Addict is a guy to chat to and how he had done some work with Tony Adams, Adams founded the Sporting Chance Clinic as a result of his own experiences with alcoholism and drug addiction. The charity provides support to current and retired athletes in three areas: education and training; one-to-one counselling (for any emotional or mental health issue); and a residential clinic set up specifically to treat addictive disorders.

Talking to Nev about mental health, I thought it would be an awkward subject, but in fact, he was very passionate whilst talking about it. Everyone feels shit. Everyone fights it, don't they? Why? But you get into a situation where you want to feel better and you feel guilty about not feeling good and you think you should be doing stuff. So all that guilt puts more pressure on you to feel even more shit. I can't get to do it today. OK, I'll do it tomorrow. Is that taking the pressure off you? He explained.

"I think sometimes we fight too much to feel good at times. Tomorrow will be a better day. The other thing is that it's far harder to stay up there (happy) than it is to stay fuckin' miserable, and I think that's why people fight. They all think everybody else thinks they should get up and have a good day, because that's what life is supposed to be, and that's what we're told it's supposed to be. " Nev continued.

Nev carried on, talking about the abuse he received when he was on the pitch. Everyone gets abuse. Everyone worries about what people think of them. Everyone does the same stuff. Once you get into that cycle, it's hard to break out. "

"It's about how you manage your feelings, but nobody ever tells the kids, or nobody tells the coaches that," Nev explained.

I totally agreed with Nev's opinion, having been through and still going through a decline in mental health. It's so easy to hide behind a smile because that's what is expected of us as human beings.

Nev explained how a player would get to the ground, say at half past one for a 3:00pm kick off, and they would feel shit. It's far easier to work your way to feeling good because you can go on and have a bit of fun.

You can work through your handling or whatever. If you get there, you'll feel great, and you've got to manage to stay up for an hour and a half. Why would you manage that for an hour and a half? That's quite difficult at times because you've got to be on that level all the time.

"If I threw you ten balls and you felt great, what's the point? But what the coaches are paid to offer, you have got to do more with him. Why? If he's ready now, what's the point? But nobody does it like that: 'you've got to do this, you've got to train for it now'.

If he feels fucking great and he's caught ten balls, brilliant. Everybody's got their own individual thing where they get to a point where they feel happy. So why not just keep them happy? "Nev continued.

Nev used to coach somebody to be like 'I always feel good', and then say "Well let's stop now". The player would think, "Oh fuck, I've got to do more.

Why would they have to do more? because the manager expected him to do more. Why would we ruin those feelings of feeling good? Why send a player onto the training pitch to save 90 shots and he comes back absolutely shattered. When somebody reaches a point where they are happy, stop it there.

Nev's point is that if you're the best you can be, then you're the happiest you can be. If you're not who you want to be, then you're never going to be happy either. He talked about how, as a footballer, you have to be yourself and you have to do what's right for you.

Sometimes you'll clash with what everybody wants to do, but fuck them because you're doing it for the right reasons. If you were just being a complete nob for the sake of being a nob, then that's different. But if you believe you're doing things for the sake of the team and yourself, it's fine. But where is that mentioned in the coaching manual?

"Everybody is slightly different; what's normal for me is not normal for you. I want to do it this way. You don't need to do it this way. Why do you want me to do it this way? "Explain to me why you don't want to," he said. I lost my brother to suicide.

Nev had opened up about isolation and loneliness and urged people to 'not stand still and stagnate', just some of the effects of mental health.

He stressed the importance of keeping active to stave off feelings of isolation as he opened up about his own experience.

"You're a man, therefore nothing's wrong with you."
"We didn't have anyone else to go to." About his feelings of isolation on the pitch, he said: "If I made a mistake in the first minute, it was a long 90 minutes and it was quite lonely."

When you make a mistake, everybody hates you.
"You can almost feel that hate, so football can be a lonely place on the pitch at times." Southall was speaking as part of a series of British Red Cross "The Kind Place" podcasts on the issue of loneliness, in conversation with 17-year-old football volunteer Kian Nash-Hill, who coaches young players in London for an education and inclusion project.

The Welsh star advised people to: "Look and learn, all the time."

"There's always somebody you can learn from, even when you feel everything's against you." "Even now, I still do courses, I still train and learn. If you stand still, either everything passes you by or you will stagnate. If you keep your mind active, I think that's the best way to do it. " Southall and Kian discussed how mental health support in football has improved in recent years, but how more can be done, especially with the absence of an openly gay footballer in the Premier League era.

Kian, who represented London county under-16s, said: "It's definitely a positive thing, just to be able to sit there and say to other people that I'm feeling this way and for everyone to take you seriously, for someone else to say: 'Yes, me too.'

"That just shows the importance of how mental health is being recognised, how everyone can support each other in the changing room."

Neville Southall joined runners at the beginning of the If You Know Your History 5k run in 2021. A huge number of Everton fans got their running shoes on again to take part in the third annual "If You Know Your History" 5km run. The event, running from St. Rupert's Tower and finishing at Goodison Park, marked a return to in-person running for Everton In The Community—with last year's race taking place virtually.

The run was, once again, raising money for The People's Place project, which will provide a purpose-built mental health facility in L4 to promote positive mental health and deliver support relating to suicide awareness and prevention.

Marking World Mental Health Day, the event saw around 600 people take part, either in person or running in another part of the world.

Neville, who started the race with a motivational message and had countless pictures taken with participants, highlighted the importance of the event in spreading positivity after what has been a tough time for the world. "It's important that people get together, especially after the pandemic, to enjoy themselves. It's supposed to be a fun run." People will chat and meet up with people that they haven't seen in a long time. They've all got the same cause in the end, to raise money for a good charity. "There's always big crowds of Everton fans. I suppose there'll be a few Reds in there as well!"

"That's what the race is about in a way. It's been so negative for such a long time, and this is a positive thing. Positive things like this are great. " When the race ended at Goodison Park, participants were encouraged to sign up to be a stem cell donor at a clinic based inside the stadium.

In 2019, £15,000 was raised for Everton In The Community. Mike Salla, Director of Health and Sport for Everton in the Community, took part in the run himself and also spoke of the huge importance of the event. He said, "It's a great day for it, even though it's a cold morning!"

It's a sign of the times. People are more confident in speaking about mental health and more open to having that conversation. The whole conversation about mental health has become more normalised, which is great. "That's the next step for The People's Place, to provide real, meaningful activities to help mental health."

It's great to have this event to celebrate mental health. A lot of talk about it from a negative point of view, but it's about people coming together and connecting. " The event has been very, very well organised. It's important people feel safe coming here and it's great to have over 600 people involved. "

Southall is educating himself on the topic of suicide awareness by studying through the Open University and attending conferences, following the release of the first national suicide bereavement report, the product of an exhaustive survey was conducted to analyse the impact of suicide on the bereaved and their experiences of accessing and using support services.

Southall shares the frustrations of the report's authors—the study was led by Dr Sharon McDonnell from the

University of Manchester—dismayed by a dearth of media coverage.

"The People's Place is brand new and has a different way of doing things," says Southall. "I am hoping it will be the centre of a spider's web, with everything coming around it to support people." If you support Everton, Liverpool, or Tranmere Rovers, it doesn't matter, does it?

It is just about helping people. "Mental health is a massive issue and a lot of things aren't working. I think we need better organisation and collaboration between universities and charities, as well as between councils and hospitals. How did the first national report on suicide not make the papers or TV? "

There is a mental health crisis all over the world. People die from suicide every day. Everton has said, "This issue is here to stay. We are going to do something about it. It will be sustainable. "

"I've not seen anything to touch Everton's community programme. Everybody has mental health. You feel good, or bad, or okay. We need to be more positive about treatment. We tend to see mental health as long-term. "Can we turn it around, like the attitude in football: 'Can you get fit for the game on Saturday?'

Sometimes, the treatment needs to be short and intense. "Let's try to get people fit as soon as possible." It's cheaper for the NHS and better for the people. Southall envisages a society where mental health centres, specialising in specific conditions, are as visible as Tesco Express. He has an idea for a 24-hour mental health radio station and wants charities regulated by the NHS and on call around the clock.

"Mental health doesn't stop when you have your tea," contends Southall, whose foster son waited six months for an educational psychologist appointment and three years for an autism diagnosis.

You can distract yourself during the day. "When you turn the lights out, your brain starts whirring."

Southall's ability to relate to 11–16-year olds with social, emotional, and behavioural difficulties was honed while playing in goal for Everton.

"In a football team, some people respond to a rollicking, others need encouragement," says Southall. "Building a relationship with the kids is no different from building a rapport with teammates.

You find common ground in something they wear, or say, or the place they come from. Everyone does it, just not always consciously. People still baffle me at times. I have no idea what makes them tick. I have learned you can't help everybody. People have to be ready to be helped, and, sometimes, it is not your turn to help them.

You have to walk away

The experience of being directly messaged by individuals at desperately low ebbs convinced Southall to broaden his knowledge of suicide.

"I've had people DM me and say they are going to do this or that," says Southall, who is investigating the possibility of being a first responder on a suicide hotline.

"That's the real side of it, where it gets quite scary for me. But that's why I've thought, if I can help through writing, can I help by talking?"

Southall remains a juggernaut of a man. "What's the point of doing a job and not trying to be the best?" – but knew when to apply the brakes.

The same is true today.

"If I need to take a break, I'll take a break," says Southall. "It is never an instant thing. I can see it building. I look for signs, so I know a week in advance I'll need a rest."

"You have to protect yourself, because it can be quite draining at times. It's no good if I'm not there tomorrow, is it? It goes back to football. If I don't feel great at 2 pm, I have one hour to work with myself to get better. If I get there and feel fantastic, where do I go from there? It is about managing how good you feel. The best I ever felt was before a game at Chelsea (in October 1985). I was buzzing in the warm-up. I did too much and got sent off. I learned from that."

"You don't want to burn all your nervous energy if you're feeling good."

If you get that, then you've got a choice. The problem is that every fucker wants something different. So you have to have a council of each group, I think, to say, "Okay, let's just see what our philosophy is and see how we want to live our lives. And I think that might be easier. It's the same as the challenges. We're trying to get some of the challenges for all the suicide charities banded together.

That's how Nev and I met, actually, because we follow each other on Twitter. We actually met through an organisation I founded, providing support for football players experiencing or having experienced mental health issues. I provided counseling and things like that. Nev actually offered for me to take over his Twitter account to promote the work that I was doing. I thought that was really an important topic.

I asked Nev, "Are you aware of the number of footballers who have taken their own lives? Do you know roughly how many?

I described how 92 footballers had taken their lives, suicides dating as far back as 1900, and how it is still happening today. Fair enough, much more is being done regarding mental health within football. The PFA and the FA now provide 24-hour hotlines for players who are in crisis. But I ask, is too little being done too late?

Neville talked about Sharon's conference, which will be held in September in Manchester. I had heard about her before and I wanted to make plans to attend this conference.

She and Nev did a 32-page document where, as a survey of men, which Nev believes is the first one ever, Sharon got 7000 men to fill it in.

It sounds like an interesting paper as Nev discussed how by the time of just one suicide, it doesn't only affect that one person. There are the family members, the ambulance, the firemen, the police, all involved in one suicide.

How many suicides today?

Nev continues, "If we're going to have suicide charities, can we work them 24 hours a day and not eight til five? Can we stagger them around the clock? When you go to A & E and somebody says, "I don't feel great, I want to harm myself," they say, "Well, we're a bit busy now. We can see you in 5 hours and the person is climbing the walls and otherwise. Excuse me, why can't you come and take this person away and have a chat? "

That would make more sense. But because of the way the funding is, everybody's shit scared of losing their funding. So they all fight for the individual funding. Instead of going, let's band together and have a voice and say, "Okay, let's do this. That, to me, will make more sense. And if you do that right, and you've got the charge, they go to the government and say, right, we want this, and they go, "No, we'll shut down for fucking three months."

See if you like that. Because without the charities, the country would come to a halt. This country runs on good people. People who take food to food banks, who contribute more to food banks, I think football fans do.

Then you have the other problem, the distribution. You have to have vehicles to distribute it. So no matter what, it all has to be really well organized. It's well organised by great people.

Nev went on to disclose how he had to fight for three years to receive a diagnosis for autism for his foster child. "My own son has just been diagnosed." I said. Nev was curious as to how long it took for him to be diagnosed. "Not too long. About a year and a half. " His own child had missed the criteria by a single point, and Nev thought it was because the government didn't want to pay him any money. I wasn't too sure if that would have been the reason for the prolonged delay, but I could certainly understand why Nev would think that.

"The way we are now, we have to change, otherwise this country is going to go tits up. This country's only running on good people, and yet the people are the ones that get shilled. Right? " Nev voiced his opinion.

"It's having a political club to change it in the first place, isn't it?" They divided the charities by funding. They divided the country by colour and gender. They divided sport, trans people by gender. I looked in the headlines the other day, the transgender clinic that shut down. If you read the headlines, you would think that it was because trans people weren't attending the clinics. But it wasn't anything to do with that. It was because the trans people were waiting too long to have treatment. The waiting list was too long.

I know the service for transgender reassignment and stuff in Sheffield is really bad. I told Nev that about seven years ago, due to what I went through with sexual abuse lasting for 13 years, it made me feel that, due to what I was forced to do during that abuse, I felt that I should have been a male, and it made me mentally unstable because of it. I actually approached a gender clinic in Sheffield.

It took three years, I think, just to get some kind of correspondence from the clinic, by which point I'd had counselling and had started on other medication, and so I felt that I didn't need the reassignment. It was just the fact that it took so long to get an answer.

"When your space is going to be safe, you can't self identify as a manner of what I'm thinking." But you're asking me to go to church every Sunday to pray to something I can't see. I've never talked to. I've never met. Whom you tell me is real, but here's this geeza who wants to change his sexuality.

You're telling me because he's here-I can't believe that can happen, but you're telling me that the Earth was raining six days because somebody made it. " I think Nev was overly passionate, if that can ever be the case, but I totally related to it all.

There's a movement to get rid of trans people, and it comes up in cycles; it dies down for a bit, then comes back up. Sports ban trans people. I'm really glad. And the reason I'm really glad is that once you ban somebody, that somebody can challenge that ban. So when it seems really negative at the moment for trans people, I'm thinking, "I see it's fucking great, because now you've got the perfect thing that you've been banned. " So I can now go and challenge that and I can do it legally.

"Whereas I don't have to just go in the paper or have a moan." I can just go and change it legally. If I change it legally, then it's going to have an outcome. It will come down to whether you're a man or a woman. Prove it. Now, if it's a case of what was on your birth date when you were born, then I'll say, overtime, nature evolves, and there are lots of animals that don't need a male, but they reproduce. " "Nature evolves."

Do humans evolve?

Nev continued to explain, "If you go back to the people who keep telling me to go to church, who made trans people? If everyone on this planet is in God's image, then he must have made trans people. If they didn't, who's making them? Are they going to say it's the devil? You can't really say it's the devil. So I just think it's why we are so fixated on what people do.

Everybody's got mental health problems. Everybody in the world has got mental health issues to a degree.

Everyone's fucking nuts in some way.

I was intrigued by Nev and his always passionate discussions. "That's what football is about." he said. "Football is about people, and they keep on showing gadgets, they keep on showing everything. And what football is about is your relationship. One person with another person, and they tell you to fit those jigsaw pieces together to make sure that you get a successful team. You have 25 egos basically living in a bubble because that's what you do. You live in a bubble. Everyone tells you what to do and when to do it. It's easier now, I think, for the players anyway, because you have social media contact."

I think that players are more aware than what they were during Nev's playing days. It was a different time and a different place.

Coping Skills

Everybody plans differently and thinks differently. The thing is, are you giving people coping skills? If you imagine now, if all your school life you were given coping strategies, would it have made a difference to you?
"I only got coping strategies at the point in my life where I really needed them." You need them all the time. I think I look back on the therapy, what I did for a specific reason, and I thought, "This is actually teaching me life skills that I could have done with all my life." It's true that if I had learned this much earlier, I would have coped with a lot of things differently. You understand your body more, you understand your mind more. "Nev continued.

I couldn't agree more with Nev as he described what should be done. We should start with primary school assemblies once a week. We give one coping strategy a week. What we normally do is say, "I tell you what, we have no coping strategies." Here's a massive exam. Pass that, and fuck off into the outside world. It's an unrealistic coping strategy. I think it's a good way of doing it.

This legend is extremely passionate about helping in whatever way he can. "I've got somebody to publish a book on this, and what we're trying to do is cover autism and coping strategies around autism." What I found is that when you go and see the GP about the illness and somebody says, "You've been diagnosed with ADHD." This is what "ADHD" is. And then the last five minutes of the appointment are, "well, let me know how you go. You've got ADHD. Look it up when you go on the internet. This is what you can do to help your kid.'" Wouldn't that be much better? But we tend not to do that.

Then the GP has to spend the next hour telling you what ADHD is and how it works in the child's head.

I talked about my own son, who was recently diagnosed with autism. Luckily, we get a lot of support in school.

When he's having a bit of a meltdown, the headteacher has made a little bedroom in an office where my son can go and get his head down for a little bit until he's feeling better, but he knows best how to cope with it himself.

"That's what we have got to get to." Nev said, "making sure you can manage yourself because you know yourself best and you know all the answers. You always know the answers. You just need to talk to somebody and talk it through. You know the answers. Everybody knows the answers. You've just got to talk it through with people and then come to that conclusion yourself. "I can sit here and talk to you until you're fuckin' blue in the face."

If you don't want to do it, you ain't going to do it. It's got to be your decision when you're ready and something that you want to do. Otherwise, you're never going to change here. No, you want to do the things that you want to do at the time.

I don't know how many friends I've had die in the last couple of weeks, and their family are crying all the time. Fucking good. That's what it's about. You're crying because as soon as it goes through you, the sooner you'll be better again. Everyone goes "Oh, I shouldn't be crying". Why not?

Don't you feel guilty about it? Just cry

If someone says, "Oh, you shouldn't be crying, he's fucking dead." What do you expect? Just let you grieve. Otherwise, if you don't, further down the line, that bereavement is going to come out in some different way. I refused to cry for many years, and like Nev said, it was going to come out one way or another.

Mine came out by attempting suicide, cutting my wrists and burning myself. But then I learned to talk about it, I told Nev, as we discussed the coping skills in detail.

Having no one to talk to at the time of a crisis could literally be a death sentence and I knew all too well. Nev asked whether a person should be relieved when somebody dies? He explained that in a strange way, he was happy when his mother passed away. "At the end of her life she wasn't the woman that I knew, so I was happy that she passed away. I knew she was in a different place, a happy place and pain free."

I would guess that a feeling of guilt but also a feeling of relief takes hold. "Relief that you know where she is and you don't have to wait for that dreaded phone call anymore. You don't walk on egg shells because you no longer think, "Is it today?" Is it tomorrow?

That weighs you down. And you think, "Okay, it's gone now. I can now finally move on." And then you go, fucking hell, should I enjoy my life? Because I do feel guilty and I was happy that she went. Although what I was feeling was perfectly natural."

That's where we don't prepare people. We don't talk about death, we don't talk about this or that. It should be about giving people the skills to cope with life.

I agreed with Nev when he said how it would make much more sense than "fucking making sure you can count".

We have all dealt with changing relationships before in our lives, from moving between schools or workplaces to beginning or ending a relationship or friendship.

These changes can help us to reflect on the past and situations where we have managed a similar challenge before. Talking about how we are feeling or our experiences with others can help us feel supported and understood.

John talked about how he and I met ten years ago via our mutual interest in mental health. We had met on a social media site. "Because of what happened to me, I got rid of my old Facebook account," John explained. "I had to get rid of it because she (his ex wife) was insane. But then I found Caz again. I told her what had happened. She'll just let me talk. She doesn't pretend to try and fix it, she just sits and listens.

I think most people know the answers; they've just got to work through them themselves.

Take John's therapy, for example. The therapist said, "We can't make you better." We'll give you the tools, but it's up to you to use them, "which is simply fine." If I just went and sat there and listened, then forgot about it until the following week, what would be the point of that? But once I got better, they're up to showing you it's inside your mind all the time, "said Nev.

You've got to be ready to accept those first steps at times. Going to therapy in the first place I think you get to a point in your life where you think, "actually, I do need help." People think it's a sign of weakness. But it's not and that's why I'm campaigning to raise awareness.

For me, having been through mental health issues, I see signs in other people, but people don't want to speak out like Nev said. They see it as a weakness, and you can see that sometimes. You'll see yourself in them.

Nev continued to explain his mental health. "I found people talking to me because I'm open now." I don't feel any shame or embarrassment. I think if people judge me in a negative way, then that's their choice. People stare at you as if to say, "He's on my fucking Twitter, and I know he saved lives."

"The thing is, people read the posts. You walk around as you are now as a visible sign that people can get through it, but you don't think about it, do you? No, you look at other people and think, "How can I help?" And actually, by you being you, you can shout from the rooftops if you want, "Nev said," as he explained how he got through his own experiences. Nev described how that could also put people off. He asked John "what you do as a job". "I work in a warehouse" John replied.

"So everybody will know your story, yeah?" They don't have to speak to you, but they know your story. They look at you, and you're not seven feet six. So you're showing your strength by walking about. So they're looking at you going, "If he can do it, I can do it." You don't realise the impact you can have on people just by walking about because they do look at you and judge.

Chapter 24
Quite simply: the UK is holding us back

I've listened to Neville, and witnessed his passion for almost everything. Poverty, I guess, is something not only myself but the wider society wants to hear about.

"Are they too poor? too small? NoAnd neither are we. It isn't a question of poverty because Wales is already poor. What's keeping it that way, do you think? When Wales regularly has a trade surplus, why are we still poor? It's the structures in place. " Nev tweeted

"I think it's an unfair country whether you live in Wales, Scotland, Ireland, or in England I think it's an unbalanced society. I think we need to get back to a fairer society where people get their basic needs met, and at the moment, if you're choosing between sanity products, toothpaste, and stuff before you eat, that can't be a good thing. So I suppose my first question would be 'where When do we start trying to address the problem?' Nev began.

With more than 11 million people in the UK living in poverty, it's one of the toughest issues in society. This is something that Neville cares very deeply about.

Nev talked to us a little bit about the kind of work that he has been doing around poverty, around his twitter account, and everything else that he is involved in.

New analysis by the Joseph Rowntree Foundation has shown the greatest fall in the value of the basic rate of employment benefit since 1972. The 3.1% increase that came into effect in April 2022 is based on inflation as of September 2021, whereas inflation was expected to hit 7.7% in May 2022. This means that households in receipt of benefits will experience a real-terms cut to their incomes, which are already at historically low levels. A Joseph Rowntree Foundation analysis has highlighted that this will put 600,000 people in poverty, around a quarter of whom are children.

"When you get universal credit, how is that based? Because you know, when you look at it, what does it cost an average person to live for a month or a week? The government or people decide on a figure or just make the figure up because universal credit seems to be the 20 quid that makes a massive difference one way or the other.

So, is there some scale they use to actually produce that number? Nev asked Andy Burnham during one of his interviews on the 90 minutes with Neville Southall podcasts. Andrew Burnham is a British politician who has served as Mayor of Greater Manchester since 2017.

"Quite simply, the UK is holding us back. More than that, as Hard Brexit looks more and more likely, the UK is endangering Wales. We only need to look at post-USSR countries like Estonia to see how much better and how fast growing our country could and will be, "Nev said.

"You look at the way your universal credit works and the way it makes people feel who are on it, it's almost designed to trip people up rather than help them, isn't it? You know, it's kind of the bureaucracy of it, the tick box nature of it, and don't forget, millions of people on universal credit are in work, so that universal credit is topping up low wages, "replied Andy.

"My thing is the carbon footprint. Obviously, we're going to have a carbon footprint or carbon footprint. So living in Wales and, obviously, there are parts of Manchester that are very rural means that you will be penalised for traveling. So that's going to impact poverty. That's why connectivity, I think, is vital to everybody, so is there anybody looking when the carbon footprint comes in or your carbon passport allows you to travel only a certain distance? I mean, I do 600 miles a week. I think in the future I'll get penalised for that. So jobs may become closer to home, and so connectivity will be a massive issue. I think by having a government outlook on the carbon footprint or carbon passport, how far would you be able to travel in the future? Nev continued. I totally understood his opinion. Would it be possible to increase carbon taxes on household energy use and transport while protecting low-income households from negative impacts?

"There's one group of people who never get mentored on the news. I've never heard any politicians talk about it. During this pandemic, sex workers must have had to go out to work. There is nowhere in the world that they cannot go out, but there was nothing done for them. Is there anything done for them or are there any schemes in place for that?

Because you know, let's be honest, they're going to get as close as they can to their clients and so the pandemic would spread. But otherwise, how would you keep them out of poverty? Because if you're asking them to stop, there's no way in the world that anybody's going to fund any of their money" Nev carried on. I had never thought about this issue and was pleased to see someone with such a passion speak out for the welfare of sex workers. Neville isn't a legend, he's much more than that.

I wanted to provide an answer of some kind to Nev, and so I carried out research into the financial support for sex workers during the pandemic. Some sex workers found their income changed during the pandemic.

If the income of a sex worker decreased, they could have been eligible for universal credit. There are some sex work specific hardship funds to support sex workers in severe financial hardship.

Self-employed people can claim up to 80% of their usual profits under the government's COVID-19 financial support. This applies to sex workers — but only if they were already registered as self-employed before the pandemic. Source

Neville asked, "How do we change the perception that people on benefits are scroungers? How do we change that way of thinking? Are the low-paid, the zero-hours, or not working at all scrounges? Because that's a perception higher up, is it? There's a perception in government that the lower you go down, the less people seem to care about you.

That you're seen as something of a lesser individual. So somewhere we've got to change that, to give people hope, to improve their mental health and make it not so much of a stigma to be on a benefit if you like. So for me, it's all about how we change perception".

Nev opened up on his views for teaching coping skills, something I teach my own children. "We never teach coaching coping strategies in school, we never make businesses make it compulsive that businesses give corporate strategies as part of their training days to businesses, you know to the employers. So for one, it's a basic thing for me.

If you want to save money through the NHS and on certain social money and the police and everything, why aren't we teaching coping strategies in schools? Why aren't we making businesses give, maybe through the mental health first aiders in work that training to people?

At least they would have some coping strategies. So what I find when I do a lot of work is that people push and push to try and find their own way and I'm saying "Well if we can give them 10, 15 or 20 different coping strategies then surely that's got to be better, so they have a range of things to try because the way things work in mental health is that to get to somebody to see somebody decent, you're talking maybe up to a year, you know. My foster kid was three years trying to get a qualification to see if he's autistic or not. So I think if we could go through schools and start with a primary school and maybe introduce coping skills through the school section, when they come out of school, they'll be miles better equipped to deal with life.

This is a perfect idea and Nev hit the nail on the head with it. I found no information showing whether schools provided such information to their pupils, I certainly know that it would have benefited my child on how to cope with his autism.

Chapter 25
Any member of your family could be doing it

I wanted to know more about the abuse Nev received because of his work supporting sex workers. "You received a lot of flack for supporting sex workers," I said.

Nev went straight into his opinionated conversations. "Sex workers, they do that work for various reasons." Why? Who am I to say that they're wrong? If I've got to feed a drug habit, for example, you can go to this place for support and you can go for that support. But no, you don't think straight, do you? "

I agree that everyone judges sex workers. You're nice and cool, you're calculating, you're calm. Yeah, you've got to find 20 quid or whatever it is to get to get some drugs because you're fucking going up the wall.

That's one of the reasons, too. Some people use it as a proper job. As I listen to Nev, my mind wanders back to the unsolved murder of a Sheffield sex worker who was stabbed to death. Michaela Hague, aged 25, was stabbed 19 times in her back and neck by a punter who picked her up for sex on Bonfire Night, 2001.

When Nev talks about how you don't know all of your family, Any of your family could be doing it. It could be somebody's brother, sister, cousin, uncle, mother, or father. People don't think of them as family. They think it's just something far away, stuck on a street corner.

Ignorance

The Chancellor of the Exchequer announced a rise in NI contributions for self-employed workers, which means sex workers pay tax just like everyone else. As that is precisely what we are, self-employed, In fact, there are specialist sex work accountants out there who know precisely what sex workers can claim for and what they can't. I wasn't very knowledgeable about the cost of being a sex worker, and so after talking to Nev about this subject, I felt I had to educate myself more on it. There are a lot of monthly expenses.

Having to pay through the nose on advertising fees (£100+), website charges (£50+), PAYG phone top-ups (£10), and using working flats (£300+). Plus, when you arrive, there's shower gel (£5), mouthwash (£5), fresh towels and clean sheets that have been laundered (£20) and refreshments (£20).

And you know what? No one ever buys their own condoms (£20 for an industrial-sized box). (This is not a euphemism.)

Also, it's handy to have a ready supply of lube (£5), baby oil (£2), tissues (£2), and wet wipes (£2). And what about those tricky little buggers who like it a little more kinky?

Nev went on to talk about the safety of sex workers. There is no statutory definition of a "brothel". However, it has been held to be "a place where people of opposite sexes are allowed to resort for illicit intercourse, whether... common prostitutes or not."

It is, therefore, not necessary to prove that the premises are in fact used for the purposes of prostitution, which involves payment for services rendered. Sections 33-35 (Section 33-keeping a brothel; Section 35-keeping a brothel; Section 34-a landlord letting premises for use as a brothel; Section 35 (a tenant permitting premises to be used as a brothel) applies to premises where intercourse is offered on a non-commercial basis as well as where it is offered in return for payment. "It is not illegal to sell sex at a brothel provided the sex worker is not involved in management or control of the brothel. A house occupied by one woman and used by her alone for prostitution is not a brothel."

"Premises only become a brothel when more than one woman uses premises for the purposes of prostitution, either simultaneously or one at a time." This implies that if two women are present, both must be there for the purposes of prostitution. In circumstances where prostitutes are working individually out of one flat but there is a rotation of occupants and the young women are moved on a regular basis, it does constitute a brothel.

Are we going to get rid of sex workers?

"There are a lot of disabled people who use sex workers. Right. And not just for sex, but for company. Yeah, I know. Honorable They go round, they have a nice little cuddle, they have coffee, and they have a really good chat. I guess that's what they want to do. " Nev explained.

"What I'm glad to see is when I'm talking to the sex workers on my podcast. They need a voice because there are a lot of them. We're judged in this country by the way we treat the most vulnerable. We treat them like shit. We treat them like animals. "

"People can debate, but it doesn't stop there, does it? It becomes personal. If you get personal abuse, somebody else ain't getting it. Why would I want to waste my time on whether they like me or not? What's really important is to be happy with yourself. If you go to bed and you're happy with yourself, that's all that matters. "

It's interesting to listen as Neville went on to discuss the welfare of sex workers. It is estimated that there are between 60,000 and 80,000 sex workers in the UK. Nev says "During this pandemic sex workers must have had to go out to work, there is nowhere in the world that they cannot go out but there was nothing done for them". Like

Nev, I am intrigued and I want to know if there is anything done in Manchester for Sex Workers or do they have any schemes in place for that?. Nev continued "You know, let's be honest they're going to get as close as they can to their clients so the pandemic would have spread but otherwise how would you keep them out of poverty? If you're asking them to stop there's no way in the world that anybody's going to fund any of their money".

Nev then talked about how as a society do we change the perception that people on benefits are scroungers. "Because that's a perception, that the lower down you go the less people seem to care about you, you're seen as something of a lesser individual. So somewhere we've got to change that to give people hope and improve their mental health and make it not so much of a stigma to be on a benefit" Nev correctly explains. I'm 100 percent behind this opinion.

It's all about how we change perception

Like any industry, it exists because there's a market for it. People want to use a brothel.

Chapter 26
You dreamed of being a professional footballer

Nev talked about disability and the challenges faced by people with disabilities. He questioned the provision of access and care. Talking via his podcast with James Rogers as well as the other members of their podcast team, Dave Feely, Keith Mullen, Mel Harvey and Simon Hart.

James spoke to Ian Biddle about disability issues and about a project in Argentina that offers university courses and internships to people with learning disabilities. A guest from a place very close to Neville's heart, Steve Johnson, is the disability manager of Everton football club. He's also been a highly successful amputee footballer in his own right. He's won three world cups with the England amputee football team, and he even achieved the accolade of world amputee footballer of the year.

Steve became a good advocate for disability. Growing up, from a young age, he was fanatical about football and played whenever he could. There were no mobile phones; it was like three channels on the television, and so all you did was play football in the street like any other young kid.

You dreamed of being a professional footballer. Steve says, "My team were Everton." I wanted to play for them, and right through school and stuff, I had that dream, but it never materialized. I wasn't picked up by Everton or any scouts, so I just played in the local league. I was a fairly decent footballer.

In 1985, I was playing football in a sports hall in Southport. The football went into the corner near the fire door and, unbeknownst to me, some rain water got underneath the fire door and I ran over to get the ball and slipped on the wet floor and went through a glass panel in the fire door, like wire glass". As Steve pulled his left leg out of the fire door, it cut all the back of his leg and cut all the nerves and veins. He knew he was in trouble. "I took my Everton shirt off and wrapped it around the wounds."

A couple of lads were sick in the changing rooms. My cousin was putting pressure on the wound to try and stem the flow of blood. An ambulance was called and I was rushed to Southport hospital". Steve recalls.

The staff tried to save his leg, but in those days it was difficult. The technology wasn't what it is now. Steve's parents made the decision to amputate his leg, which was difficult for them because they knew how much Steve loved playing football.

Steve saw the ambulance drivers a couple of weeks later and they said "you know, we thought you weren't going to make it". "I've always tried to look at it as a positive thing really with regards to, you know, you're still here, you can still do whatever you want to do," Steve explained.

Steve tried playing football again, but it was really difficult and he went from being able to play football whenever he wanted to having no football opportunities as a disabled person.

Steve visited a centre for disability sports and was disappointed because there was no football at the time. He actually took up volleyball and started playing volleyball, joining two mainstream teams and getting into the Great Britain Disabled Volleyball team. "I was lucky enough to go to two paralympics and the world championships," he said.

In 1987, a guy came over from America and introduced amputee football to Stoke Mandeville. Steve took to it straight away. "I've never really thought about it, but after taking my leg off and playing with crutches, I was so mobile on it. It was a breath of fresh air. There was a group of us who got together in the north west of England and started playing football regularly every week. We were invited to the World Cup in America the following year.

Obviously, I went on to win three world cups and travel all over the world.

Nev asked Steve, "How did you cope mentally?" I mean, you were pretty young when you did it, so how did you cope mentally? And do people come to you and ask you how to cope mentally? Neville was curious about people approaching Steve. "Do amputees come up to you asking for advice?" he asked. "As I mentioned before, I looked at it as I am still here. I can still do whatever I want to do.

You know, I always looked at it as a positive kind of thing, but it's obviously not the same for everybody else. Other people struggle to come to terms with losing a limb and becoming disabled. So, starting the football, it wasn't just about playing football, it was about being a support mechanism for other players, "explained Steve.

With the mental health care, some of the players joined the team not necessarily to play football but for that support kind of thing. Back in 1985, there wouldn't be that much support around for amputees. It was difficult for them.

"What were the laws on first aid like around that time? You said you did it at a leisure center. Nowadays, they always have first aid, good insurance, and all the risk assessments, "asked Nev."

Steve told Nev how it was different back in those days. There would be no risk assessments and no first aiders. There was nothing in the sports industry, nothing at the youth club, it was just non-existent. After Steve's accident, they were supposed to take all of the glass out of all of the sports centres to stop that from happening again.

Nev listened intently as Steve explained how his experiences shaped the way he now works in his work with Everton and their disability programs.

"It gave me inspiration to do something I wanted to do, which has changed the situation with regards to there being "no football opportunities for disabled people", so I wanted to change that. I applied for jobs in disability sports, but it was difficult to get them. I had to go to university as a mature student because that was the only place that did disability sports studies.

I did that and then completed a degree. I was really fortunate at that time because the English Federation of Disability Sport was just starting a new project called the 'One to One Ability Council Program', which was trying to encourage football clubs to take on people with disabilities through their community programs," Steve explained.

Steve and Glenn Keeley (an English retired footballer who played as a central defender in the Football League) went round to 50 different clubs, signing 50 clubs up. The clubs started providing regular football opportunities for disabled people, and this was the first time any grassroots programme had started. It was really innovative. Everton was one of the first clubs to get involved.

Steve explained to Nev how a job became available at Everton Football Club back in 2003, and he has been at Everton ever since. Originally, it was about giving disabled people the same football opportunities as non-disabled people, but the actual work that Steve does through his programme has changed and gone off on different tangents.

Chapter 27
That's why I've got a real problem with the LGBT thing

Neville received a lot of abuse because of his support for the LGBT community. He was accused of being gay. People said he slept with trans women and sex workers. It was even said that he retired from football as he had no time to fit it in between all of his other stuff. One fella tried to come up with an intelligent, considered reply to Nev, but he said, "I keep coming back to this." Fuck em ".

Sarcastically, a typical reply from Nev was, "The problem is a lot of people think I already have." But I get what you mean.

I understand people who don't think someone can stand up for someone else unless they have a vested interest. I believe it's a lack of education, a lack of understanding.

But where is the compassion, shared humanity? I was glad to see Neville standing up for those whom others would knock down. People will attack and insult people like Nev who help the vulnerable. Nev is saving people who struggle. That's a big thing. It's obvious that Nev's presence on Twitter has saved people's lives.

"Do you want kids to be the best? All you want is to reach your full potential. Is it not what anybody wants? And that's why I've got a real problem with the LGBT thing, because people have to hide at times, and they have to hide who they are. They never reach their full potential.

So you look at the Premier League now. There must be a policy, but how could the players be themselves? How could they be the best they could be? Because they're always hiding, "Nev said during our meeting.

"To me, that is criminal. What we should be doing is letting everybody reach their full potential. Otherwise, what's the fucking point? We only want to be the best we can be and be the happiest we can be. Because if you're not who you want to be, then you're never going to be happy either. So the first thing is to make sure that everybody can be who they want to be and then go from there.

I told Nev about my own story, how I came out to my family at the age of 21. Although I had actually come out years before to a few friends, I hid it from my family. A school friend and I lost contact after leaving school back in 1996. We bumped into each other on a bus in 2001. I was weeks away from giving birth to my third daughter, and Michele became my method of support. Ten weeks after giving birth, I decided to Michele that I was bisexual. I sent her a text message: "Pidge, I'm gay.. well, I'm bi-sexual," it read. She texted back, 'Me too'. The rest is history.

"You can't have people hiding for this and that. It just causes grief when there's no need to cause grief. And again, if you go by LGBT, I can't see a plan for when people come out, "Nev said. They're going to get done by one of the Sunday papers. That's not a nice way to come out. But I do think to be a footballer, you have to be yourself and you have to do what's right for you.

Sometimes you'll clash with what everybody else wants to do, but fuck them because you're doing it for the right reasons. If you were just being a complete knob for the sake of being a knob, then that's different. But if you believe you're doing things for the sake of the team and yourself, I think that's fine. But where did they mention that? In the coaching manual? "Nev continued.

Everybody is slightly different. What's normal for me is not normal for you. I want to do it this way. You don't need to do it this way. Why do you want me to do it this way? Explain to me why you don't want to.

"Football coaches should go on courses covering LGBT, bullying, racism, insurance, safeguarding and all of those things before they can teach any sport in Wales." And I think that will take the pressure off the sports themselves. " Nev went on. I agreed with him. The game needs any member of the coaching/managing staff to be aware of these issues and the potential risks to players who are classified in these bands.

"What I hate is these rainbow laces. (THE rainbow laces campaign is football battling homophobia in British sport. The campaign aims to raise awareness and support for lesbian, gay, bisexual and transgender players and fans). It is one of the things I don't like. Because it's like they are saying, "I'm gay this weekend." What about the rest of you?' 'I'm not gay, then I'm black this weekend' and so on. Nev said.

I wanted to push Nev on this subject. "So, what do you think about this taking the knee on the pitch? Do you have the same opinion that we think that's not quite right? I asked.

"Well, my opinion is I'm totally for everybody, but sometimes I think some of these things actually stir up more trouble than this old 'there's a way for me'. I mean, we had the Kick It Out thing (Kick It Out is an organisation fighting discrimination.

They're here to make sure football is a game for everyone – and that means putting equality and inclusion up front). That's just my opinion. Sometimes things that are intended to bring people together actually end up being dividers.

At least people are talking. "I think sometimes when they take the knee, there are two ways of looking at why they have to take the knee in the first place. Okay, so there's a reason-they continually take it because the FA aren't strong enough in what they're doing (and I don't think they are). But the other reason is, I think when you go and play in Hungary or places where the black players get enormous amounts of abuse and they're all promised all this shit that's going to happen, how would you protest? I think taking it is a good thing. Not every team did it. I'm not sure if any women's teams did it either, which I found strange. There was no explanation why they didn't do it. "Nev continued.

John explained how he attended two football games. At one game, the players took the knee; at the other game, they didn't.

I think sometimes you need something to create that debate or conversation. I think that's why rainbow laces serve a purpose. Some of the players don't wear them. I think it's better to stir up stuff. In this country, nobody talks about LGBT people, especially trans people, because we never had discussions about them because as soon as you say, "well, I think this", you're fucking homophobic, let's just have a proper debate. Honestly, I believe this, right?

There's fucking tonnes of infighting about the LGBT stuff. We should do a lot of infighting. I do think they should. It's not a problem for the government because they love it. But it's a big problem for LGBTQ+ people, I think, because no matter what work you do, you have got that one voice where we're talking to a million people. Yeah, a million people. For a government, it's hard work.

Neville Southall is far more famous for standing up for people without a voice in mainstream society than for standing up to attackers bearing down on his goal. "You need to have things that spark debates, but you also need your government to be brave enough to have the debates."

I never met a gay person in my life until I left football, but I must have. But then you're in the dressing room, and nobody ever really sat down and said, "Oh, he's got to be this and he's got to be that." So I never met anybody. Then I looked at this thing and it said, "Bi AF." So I tweeted the girl. I said, "what is AF?" ""As fuck, you idiot," she replied.

Listening to Nev talk so openly about his views, I couldn't help but think back to a comment my father made not long after I had come out as gay. "It doesn't matter where you go, you've brought it on yourself". My father was referring to the homophobic abuse me and Michele had been receiving. It had got to a point where we wanted to relocate and live somewhere else.

I grew up playing football myself, so I know the culture surrounding the sport is very homophobic and transphobic. So I have huge respect for Nev for using his position and status to speak out against such things, knowing the backlash he would get.

[I didn't like who I was as a footballer. Looking back, I didn't like what I was. Now, it's a lot easier to be who I want to be and who I am because I'm not a performing dog anymore. I don't have to be what I needed to be then. What I needed to be then was the best I possibly could be, to the detriment of most of the other things in my life. Now I don't have to do that; it's a far easier life and I'm far happier.]

"I don't like the word LGBTQ+. It should be a softer word. It is that reputation, forged over three decades on the football field, that means that Southall is listened to. He is at Wembley as a patron of the LGBT group Just A Ball

Game at their first-ever seminar called Stronger Together, the culmination of a lifetime's work by their founder, Lindsay England, a tireless campaigner for equality in all fields. In England, Southall has met a kindred spirit.
I worked with Lindsay for a brief spell and was captivated by her passion for the work she did.

"I met Lindsay through Twitter. What I like about Lindsay is that she just grafts and grafts and grafts. She doesn't get much funding. She's always looking for new funding, always keen to promote it. I think when you've got people like Lindsay, LGBT people have got a chance at succeeding in football, "explains Nev.

Southall's passion for LGBT issues stems from when a boy he was teaching in Ebbw Vale came out. "In the process," you think, "how am I ever going to be able to speak to this kid?" What do I actually know about LGBT stuff? Nothing.

I didn't think I knew anyone who was gay at that time, but I must have, and I must have played with someone who was gay, by sheer averages. I contacted a few people on Twitter and they've been brilliant. They gave me good advice.

"What I didn't realise until I finished football is the impact that your words can have on people. Your words do have an effect, and I think sometimes you have got to sit back and realise what words can mean. I think that one of the things is that if you use the "N" word (in football), you get sent off; if you call someone a "queer", you don't get sent off. I think that's wrong. I think that should be addressed. Why is one different from the other? Both words are the same. "

"It seems to me that sometimes the FAs want to tick off stuff. You can't just tick boxes." Tell me about an FA Cup Final or one of the other finals in which you had anything to do with LGBT people. These are our show-pieces, and yet we don't do anything. When you have "Rainbow Laces Day", have the ball, the referee, the corner flags, the nets, the mascot, stuff around the ground all in rainbow colours, have workshops around the grounds, so you're actually meeting people. If we're going to host something, it's no good going to talk to people who are already converted. The people who you want to get out are the fans on the terraces. "

Why can't we show the world that we're taking it seriously instead of going "we'll have a talk"? I'd love to see the stewards trained properly and have cameras on their tops like the police do. I'd like them to film the people and get them banned for life. You can't just play on, you've got to stop it. If you don't stop it, it's going to carry on. What are we saying? We're saying this is wrong and if you say it, you're out and you don't come back. We need to lead by example.

Neville has for some time been an advocate for Lesbian, Gay, Bisexual, and Trans+ inclusion and agreed to take on the straight ally ambassador role to help take an important stand for the LGBT+ community by joining the campaign against homophobic, biphobic, and transphobic (HBT) bullying in football and other sports.

Southall champions the cause of both the Bradford City LGBT+ fan group and JBG? stating: "I think it's important that the football community and the LGBT+ community talk more, and maybe I can help."

"I think it's only a matter of time that a footballer will come out," he says. "With the work of charities like Just A Ball Game? We hope to make it a better environment to help that happen. On Twitter, Southall posted: "If you're gay, straight, trans, or anything else, you should be able to be what you want (not live a lie) without discrimination or prejudice."

The messages that JBG? sends out are very much a big YES to equality, inclusion, and diversity and a big NO to 'HBT' abuse or bullying.

The Founder of JBG?, Lindsay England, welcomed the involvement of the ex-professional as, "A fantastic addition to the LGBT+ and straight alliance for both our JBG? educational campaign work and raising the profile of the LGBT fan group at Bradford City."

"Football faces some tough challenges ahead not just at top level but at grassroots where gender and sexuality issues need clear and equal rules". The player said he is "privileged" to now work so closely with gay people.
As the years have gone by, I have been privileged enough to meet many people who are gay, and some of them I am now lucky enough to call good friends," wrote the footballer.

"If I had been born a woman in a man's body, and I told everyone I was a woman, I think I would have gotten a different response altogether, and not a positive one. But if I knew that was what I was inside, then what was the difference? " He added

"We're delighted that Neville has agreed to become a patron of the Rainbow Toffees," said founding member Dr Mike Homfray.

"We look forward to working with one of our club's greatest ever players as he helps us raise awareness of LGBT issues in sport and improve acceptance of who we are in the football community."

Neville talked to me about the impact of LGBT ignorance within the game. "They're going to leave people out of the European Championships and the World Cups because it's going to be a separate super league." So once the World Cup and the European Championships are over, I suppose the Women's Premier League will keep going, but will Sky pull out of the Premier League to go to the Super League? I think that in time, all the big primary teams won't be any part of Sky, BT, Amazon, or anybody. They'll have a stream themselves and they'll sell their own stuff.

They'll make their own money because they can afford to do it. "Football's got big changes," said Nev. It made me wonder if the so-called modern era is actually modern at all. Could what Nev said actually happen?

"There will be the gay Premier League player whenever, so it'll be a stepping stone for the next few and then they'll become normal and after gay people become normal, then there's going to be the big question around trans people." Nev continued

"The sports have a lot going on, some big decisions to make, and it's quite fascinating. I think the transition will take at least ten years. But to take it through the high court and stuff, you know. If you self-identify as a female in the workplace or you're treated as a female, then you're seen as a woman. "

"One of the trans girls I spoke to went into work as a female. They knocked ten grand off of her wages because she's female, not male. So the boys will get ten grand more. Which highlights another problem. Somewhere along the way, you need to have a proper debate about stuff, don't you? "

Rather than just guessing shit, I think that's what people tend to try and do. But at the moment, it's definitely a swing towards eradicating trans people. But it shows a different issue for a trans woman to go into one space than sex trafficking.

Because that's why I get accused of sex trafficking and not liking women. It's just fucking ridiculous. And women want safe spaces. So what is a "safe space?" "It can be a safer space, but it can't be a safe space.

Unless you're stuck in a room on your own, surrounded by three foot thick walls and the door to which only you have the key to serve as your safe. That's not how people want to be, is it? They want to be free and walk around. "

What Nev said next caught my attention. "Why aren't there any alarms on mobile phones for women? For men? for their safety. Because that's what most people carry around these days, phones.

"So why isn't there just a button you can press where it can direct you straight through to me? I've been trying to talk to a couple of people about when you buy a phone. Every new phone comes with an app such as the Samaritans app on it. If you just did it in one area to begin with. "

Is there an option to get an alarm put on the phone? Or could somebody put an alarm on the phone because you have got trackers on them, but you don't want tracking. Everything goes through your phone eventually. So why not just build an alarm that will sound if the button is pressed?

I was interested in this idea; it was an idea I wanted to pursue. I made a note of that for when I got home. The kind of ridiculous thing Nev receives and doesn't understand is that there's someone who just kept going on about the toilets. "Would you like your daughter to go the toilets with a transmale?". "' I certainly said that myself. A person is gay, so there must be all these terrible things.

Who gives a fuck? The main people who run the concierge are so worked up about shit. You can't talk about that. Why not?

What they don't realise is that how do you address LGBTQ+ people? I'm sure they should be called something something different, something nicer, softer. Because it's a long word, LGBTQ+

"Rainbow people are easier," Nev said. Being honest, I said that Rainbow people remind me of the cartoon Rainbow with George and Bungle. It doesn't describe what people actually are.

What is the plus in LGBTQ?

"All the other things." There are plenty more, aren't there?"

It's funny because at first, a guy thought I was transgender because of the Twitter Takeover. I suppose it wasn't explained properly. The takeover is about somebody else taking over my Twitter account to promote their own issues, charities, etc. During the first few weeks, people thought I was suicidal. So it took a little while for people to get used to the takeovers.

Southall is even more animated when discussing homophobia in football. "I did a thing for the Rainbow Toffees [Everton's LGBT supporters' group]. It was great and it made me think the FA took the piss with their LGBT relations day.

Will you wear some rainbow laces one day?

Is there anybody in the commentary team that's within the LGBT community? "No." Have you talked to any players? "No" Do you have any LGBT people on the pitch? No, "I said to them," I wanted Everton to be the first club to get their LGBT people on at half-time and play a five-a-side. Arsenal wanted to play us. I thought we might get some stick. But I'm hoping Everton fans are sensible and people get used to it. " Nev said.

"Will a gay Premier League footballer come out soon? Yes, because the press will out him. The Sun said they wouldn't name that bisexual footballer because they didn't think it was right. Fuck off. He probably got an injunction. But the first gay footballer will be a multimillionaire. The problem is that the FA is not proactive. I spoke to a gay referee and he said if you use the N-word you get sent off. If a fan says it, he's thrown out of the ground. But you don't get sent off or chucked out for using a derogatory homophobic term," explained Nev."

Away from football, Southall's disdain for the Conservative government is plain. The day May killed me was when she spoke about 'JAMs'—people who are Just About Managing. I used to think she'd be a bit more compassionate, but she's colder than all the others. "

Southall supports Labour, even if they frustrate him, and he says: "Jeremy Corbyn's done all right." Whether you like him or hate him, he sticks to what he says. When he was made leader, people took the piss because he didn't wear a suit. Well, he's not Clark Kent. I thought: "If he doesn't look like a politician, great." I don't want a One of Southall's trademark Twitter witticisms has centred on bizarre jokes about skeletons, which mock the Tories' austerity cuts.

"That started because I was asked to talk at some function for funeral directors in Croydon. I thought: 'What the fuck do I say?' I started talking about skeletons, and it was a funny night. I said maybe we could replace lampstands with skeletons. It would be nice to have your uncle sit there in the lounge as a coffee table. "

After a few engaging and surreal hours, Southall stays on to talk even when the tape is off. He tells me, movingly, about the two foster children he and his wife look after, and he finds new energy when compiling a list of people he wants me to contact.

I feel even more uplifted when, in the following days, quotes pour in from some of those to whom he has offered a Twitter platform. Appreciation of Southall's generosity and openness illuminate their messages. But Jessa Jones, a sex worker, makes a telling point. "I was surprised that the first thing Neville asked upon learning what I do for a living was: 'What do sex workers want to make their lives better?'" Jones reveals.

"In the face of such fierce eloquence, I can imagine Southall nodding and smiling, happy that the final words of this interview are not his own.

Chapter 28
You're asking me?

So, I had no prepared questions. I wanted the interview to be original, and it certainly ended up that way. I said to Nev that if he answered questions from Chapter 13 of my book "You're Asking Me," then I would have a tattoo of the figure I had just given him as a gift.

"I'm going to ask you lots of random questions." I don't know where to start. Shall I start with chapter 13? "I asked.

Whatever, where do you want to start? I thought you would have a list of questions already, "Nev said."

"I didn't want to ask boring questions." I didn't want to be like anybody else.

OK, let's start with the Chapter 13 questions. "Start where you want to start, you'll either get a yes or a no," he said. "What would you do if a man had difficulty with premature ejaculation?" I asked.

"Send them to the fuckin' doctor," Nev answered. "Do you have a preference between sex in the morning or at night?"

"No." No preference" he laughed. "I never know where I'm going to be". "Basically, get it whenever you can" I joked. "It has to be spontaneous," Nev joked back. "So why are you missing the afternoon".

"Morning or night? Well, it is just a question. I said, whilst Nev blushed. "That's saying nobody wants sex in the afternoon," he laughed.

"I don't know about that. Whenever you can. "I'm not really bothered to be honest, one way or the other. Can you predict how I will wake up in the morning? "My lifestyle would suit the night rather than the morning," he explained. "What do I prefer, if the other person doesn't? "Given your current sex drive, how often would you like to have sex with your spouse?" I continued. "Well, I can't really respond to that, can I?" Whatever my sex drive is, you can't just do it because it's a chore, can you? It's got to be that you both want to do it, "Nev went on." "Isn't there two people having sex, not just one?"

I joked, "It could be sex on your own".

You can't force yourself on somebody. It's got to be a mutual thing, isn't it? Nev asked.

"Definitely." Yeah, All right. Move on to the next question. "What is the dumbest way you've been hurt?" I asked. "Dumbest way I've been hurt?" Once, I bent down to pick up a stick, and the stick went into my eye. I had to go to the hospital for that. It wasn't nice. I scratched my eyeball.

I knocked on somebody's door once when I was a kid and then ran. I was trying to jump over this little tiny fence. I ran and tripped on the fence post and it went in my fuckin ear, "he described.

"Oh my god," I said.

Yeah, but in those days, you didn't call for an ambulance. I had to walk up to the fuckin' hospital with my mum with a flannel on my head. I had six or seven stitches in my head. Or the time when I jumped up to try and stick a knife in a tree. What I should have done was to have the knife blade facing down, but I had it facing up. The blade went down my finger.

Would you say you're a bit of a calamity? Accident prone? Away from football?

"No, not at all," Nev continued. "Are you sure?" I joked. "Maybe I was when I was a kid." I just bump into stuff now. "he laughed. "There you go, calamity," I responded with amusement.

"Yeah, but that's not because I'm clumsy." That's because I'm thinking of something else. "

I laughed and joked, "Sex in the afternoon?".

"You have met some awesome people, haven't you? "I've never really met anybody where I've said 'fuckin' wow. Because people are people, aren't they? Unless they are arse holes.

"What certain product can't you live without?" I continued. "A kettle, that's it. Anything else, I can get by without. You've got to have a cup of tea, haven't ya? "Nev said.

"How often do you replace your bed sheets?"

"Every week. What did you mean to replace? Ones to wash? They are washed once a week. Nev answered.

"I bet you didn't expect questions like this," John joked.

"I could go back to Chapter 13." I laughed.

"Do what you want; it seems you're obsessed with it anyway," said Nev.

"People don't understand this, but I am actually diagnosed with Persistent Sexual Arousal Disorder," I explained. (Persistent genital arousal disorder (PGAD) is a phenomenon in which afflicted women experience spontaneous genital arousal, unresolved by orgasms, and triggered by sexual or nonsexual stimuli, elicits stress. "Okay, You do know whether you're coming or going then? Good comeback. I realised just then how awesome this guy is and how down to earth he can be.

"Is it difficult for you to ask your wife, should I say, for certain kinds of stimulaltion?". Nev didn't want to answer this question but he did say he wouldn't be shy to ask anybody anything. After all, it is nature, isn't it? A lot of people are shy.

"If you're married to somebody and living with somebody, how could you be shy? Nev asked.

"Quite easy. My wife, I wouldn't dream of saying stuff to her because she's really, really shy, "I said

"No, that's not, sometimes it's just communication problem isn't it? "What does shy mean?" Nev asked. Shy? I don't know. If I asked my wife to perform oral sex, she would blush. She would wish for the earth to just swallow her up. I'd say that's being shy. I tried to explain

Nev wasn't really sure how to answer, "I don't know what shy means." Your wife may feel awkward. But does she feel awkward because she doesn't want to do it or because of the fact that you've asked in a certain way? Otherwise, is it the way she was brought up and so it could be the way you ask "

"Then I assume that you don't ask in that way because you know the answer to start with."

"Now you get my mind working," I said.

Obviously you've got to communicate with your partner. So if you walk in the bedroom and say right, do this and she doesn't like it that way, but you're clever enough to know that, so you don't ask her that, do you? Otherwise, I'd say you have a communication problem, but you have it because you want to get what you want to get and she wants to do it. But it's just a way of finding a way of asking. You probably don't ask, you probably just guide.

At this point during the interview, I realised that I'd met my match. Nev had achieved the impossible; he made me blush, and I never ever blush. I was stuck for words.

"That's why you communicate, to get what you want the best way you can. She does the same thing. You find the middle ground. That's why you're married.

"What physical or personal trait do you think makes people first attracted to you?

"I don't know, I never worry about it," he answered. I told him it was his eyes. "That's for you to decide. Not for me to decide. Somebody might look at my legs or my arse. How am I supposed to answer that?

"It's the first time I've ever seen Nev from the front. I've always seen him from the back, "laughed John.

"What would make me attractive to a female or a male? Nev said. I asked him if there was any part of him that he thought would attract a person.

To be honest, I don't give a fuck. Seriously? I don't ever think about it. Why should I think about it? I've got my wife and that's it, "Nev answered."

"What does your wife find attractive?" "About me?. Fuck knows, I've no idea". "It's this communication problem," I joked.

"No, I think it's humor". Nev carried on.

"Humor? You are very humorous. When you go home you've got to ask her if she finds you humorous" I said. I couldn't stop myself from laughing as Nev said his wife finds him funny, but he wasn't sure if she found him funny as in comical or as in lunacy. He said she had a great sense of humour and he laughed at her too.

"Anymore ridiculous questions?" aked Nev.

"I've got tons. Do you want me to keep asking?" So I continued firing questions. "Do you feel that you need to be occasionally held or emotionally supported by someone?

"I think you wouldn't be human if you didn't" Nev answered, I felt that Nev was trying to avoid such a personal question and talked in the sense of other people.

"This is for you. Do *you* need emotional support? Do you need a hug at times?" I asked.

"No, I don't need a hug. I think it's nice to have contact but I like to know my wife is in bed, I like to touch my wife and have that contact but otherwise, I don't need someone to give me a fuckin' hug".

"Who wrote this book? Fuckin' Doctor Freud? Nev joked. "A perverts guide to relationships. Is it? he continued as he referred to "You're Asking Me?, another book I wrote.

"That is so weird because he (John) calls me a colossal Pervert" I joked.

"I've never met anyone like her" replied John.

"Right. A couple of things and then we'll let you go" I laughed as John joked with Nev saying that Nev could get up and leave the interview at any time if he had had enough.

So, I fired some random questions, mainly jokes, actually. Just so I could express Nev's true humour.

"Right. Which room has no walls?

"Huh?"

Which room has no walls? It's a joke. "

"Is it?"

"Yeah, which room has no walls?" I repeated

"A mushroom".

"Where is an ocean with no water?" I asked. "The moon," answered Nev. "A map".

"An ocean with no water is a sea bed, technically, if there's no sea," Nev replied. I was really starting to see his humour, and I loved it.

I'm heavy forward, but backwards I'm not. What am I? I asked. "Time," he replied. "A tonne".

Nev began asking me questions. I wasn't expecting that. "Here's a question for you," he said. If you were stuck in a jail cell, right? No windows, it's four feet of concrete, right? All that is in the room is a table. They locked you in. The door is five feet thick. How'd you get out? "

"So there are no windows, only a table and a door," I repeated. "So this is one of your stupid ones. You should pop this in your book here, "replied Nev.

"You cut the table in half like a hole, and you crawl out the hole". Nev laughed.

You donut, "I said. Nev continued to banter.

"So the worst thing is you don't get it".

"I do get it!" I laughed.

Well, is there anything you personally want to talk about? I asked, having asked everything I wanted to ask.

"I thought you were asking a question. I honestly thought you would come with a list of questions, "replied Nev. "I didn't expect to discuss wanking and that kind of stuff, did I?"

I asked Nev about the amount or lack of media articles that are on the internet about Neville wanking, in which he said there were none. I think this proved my point to Nev that I wanted our interview to be unique.

Nev took the book and began reading the questions. "Have you ever experienced being confined in a hospital?" he read. "Has anyone tried to kill you?" he continued to read. "What kind of fucking question is that?" he asked. It was a little ironic that Nev asked those two questions, what with John's situation. "You picked those two out for me," John joked.

But these were, after all, just random questions!

"How do you think I could handle myself when I'm in a crisis situation?" Nev read aloud.

Typically, Nev didn't give a straight answer and began to question what the meaning of that question was.

"It was saying how you think I would handle myself. That means I'm asking myself if I'm asking that question. How do you think I would handle myself when I'm in a crisis situation! "," said Nev, boggling my mind with this now confusing question.

"If someone tells you a juicy tip about a friend or coworker, do you have difficulty keeping it to yourself? Do you ever tell people they shouldn't gossip? " Nev kept going through the questions in what now appears to be an inappropriate book. "That's a fucking definite no for you," he said to me.

I seriously don't know what impression I gave Nev, but his sense of humour was fantastic.

"To be honest, I think he's pretty much got a measure of you," John replied. I'll ask the expert. "He knows you better than I do," said Nev. I told him how cheeky he was becoming.

"People from Sheffield, you just want people to say what you want them to say," Nev continued. It's a Yorkshire thing, isn't it?

"I prefer you to say what you want to say, honest opinions," I responded.

"If your family hated the person you were dating or marrying, would you get married anyway? Did you come up with these questions? "nev asked.

"The majority of them, yes," I replied, laughing.

Nev continued to grill me. "If you were a spy, who would you like to poison?

(I could easily answer that one, but I chose not to).

"If you became Prime Minister of your country, what would you do to change it?"

"I would love to be Prime Minister," I said. "Would you? ", "I would. I'm not even going into that with you, "I said, knowing that if I did answer that question, it would open up a whole new chapter of opinions.

"So what would be the first thing you change?" Nev asked anyway.

"Public services".

"In what way?"

I knew I was heading towards disaster by keeping this question open. But I chose to carry on anyway. "Well, we need more cops on the streets, we need NHS workers, and we definitely need better mental health services. I think a lot of the services have been cut down". Nev interupted, "Who's paying for all these services?"

"Yeah, exactly," is what I thought. How would you pay for it? "Tax all the rich fuckers!" Nev answered his own question.

Chapter 29
Famous quotes

"You don't expect loose cannons to take over your own country.

Q: Do you have a favourite save?
A: No, it's my job. Does a postman have a favourite letterbox?

"I'm quite scatty. I'm not neat and tidy and I don't like being enclosed by four walls. "

We seem to have a real problem in this country with saying that we're struggling. We seem to have a real problem saying we need help.

"If you sit there and think 'I'm good,' then you don't improve, do you?"

"When you look into a person's eyes, you see the real them. Someone with a million secrets is struggling along, trying to cope as best they can. Humans"

"If I changed 100 things and got 1% better because of one of them, then it was worth it."

"If the Evertonians took to you, you had won over a section of people who lived in an environment where they judged harshly. And why not? They expect the best. "

"My Everton #41: Evertonians' acceptance is all I need."

On the demands of playing for Everton

"At Everton, they want you to play your b******* off every game. They don't care if you've had a row with your missus, or if you don't feel that well, or if you're not quite fit. They don't care about any of that. You've got to be perfect, and if you're not, they don't like you. "

Backing former teammate Duncan Ferguson for the Everton manager's job this summer

"It's important to support Big Dunc. "He's the only man since Joe Royle to show the loyalty and dedication to revive our fantastic club's fortunes." He has stepped up each time he has been asked with pride, passion, commitment, and drive to help our beloved club. If anyone understands the club, it is him. We have tried all sorts of managers and in different ways, they have all come up short. "The big guy has learned a tremendous amount from each one, but now I feel it's his time to become the manager."

On not attending the traditional FA Cup final banquet after Everton's 1-0 victory over Manchester United in 1995

Stubbs: "Neville, you've produced some magnificent performances in your day, but those saves in the second half, surely they must be among the best you've ever made?"
Southall: "Not really, no."
(loud laughter from teammates standing beside him)
Pauses : "It's a team game, it's a squad game, and they all pulled their weight today, and I think we thoroughly deserved to win the game, and it shows what a good side we really are."
Stubbs: "Now will you go to the team banquet this evening? Will you join in the celebrations?"
Southall: "No, I'll go home."
Stubbs: "You've got to stay after a performance like that, surely?"
Southall: "When you've been with these lads as long as I have, you'll want to go home as well!"

On Scousers (from The Binman Chronicles)

"They're a bit special. They've all got really good hearts. They're quite aggressive because it's a hard city and you have to fight for what you want, sometimes just to earn a living. They're determined. They have a great sense of humour as well as some class.

To Michael Owen, after Liverpool and England's star striker at the time, shouted "get in there!" after scoring past a schoolboy goalkeeper in an instructional football training video the pair were taking part in

"Well done, he's 13."

In the half-time sit-down incident in 1990, when, with Everton trailing 2-0 at home to newly-promoted Leeds United, he came back out to the pitch early and leant against a goal post.

"People thought that I had come out to make a point about my transfer request and that I'd sat down to make my feelings clear. " That had nothing to do with it whatsoever. We didn't have the best of first halves. After all that had gone on last season, which to be honest wasn't one of our best, the last thing I wanted was to start off in the first league game with a bad defeat. " During the pre-season games, I received some nasty comments from one or two people because of the transfer situation. " Some even said that they would be happy if I broke my leg. "I felt I had something to prove and I wanted to do well against Leeds for the fans, the manager and the rest of the players." When you want something so badly and it goes to pieces, possibly because you're trying too hard, then there's a chance something will give.

On working as a binman (from The Binman Chronicles)

"Being a binman is something people always remember me for, but I actually only worked the bins for a couple of months." Although the first few 4:30am starts were a struggle, and I had to get wise to the rest of the crew sending me to go and get the bins at houses with big dogs – I'd always be getting chased by dogs in the first few weeks – it suited me down to the ground. "We'd stop for breakfast halfway through, and I'd be finished by 10am."

He plays for the boss he considers to be the worst.

"I don't like Alan Partridge because he managed me under the name of Mike Walker. Not funny then. "

On his work now, both in a special-needs school and his social activism online

"I've got the best of both worlds. I've got a background where I've got respect and trust from the older generation, but I'm also building relationships with younger people through what I do with my work. I like people to judge me for who I am and not what I was. "Football has taught me that you have to deal with lots of different kinds of individual personalities."

On his stunning and crucial save in the 1984/85 title race from Tottenham's Mark Falco (from The Binman Chronicles)

"What more can I say? It was straight at me and I've saved plenty like that on the training ground. " I always knew I was going to get it. My teammates certainly didn't congratulate me. " (Kevin) Ratcliffe yelled at me: "Why didn't you catch it? Why are you f****** giving a corner away?'

Chapter 30
Practical Joker

It's easy to imagine what kind of antics Nev got up to in his days on the pitch, or should I say, behind the scenes.

Nev has memories of Everton and Wales... diarrhoea, stolen lamps and winding up Martin Keown

Nev talks about his love for fun in the dressing room.

"I'll bet footballers have missed their dressing rooms during the shutdown. They tend to be funny places, and it's good to laugh sometimes, "he says."

Nev described his days as a teenager playing for Llandudno Swifts. "I remember us driving all the way to Düsseldorf in a bus which probably wouldn't pass an MOT – it broke down just before we got there. On our first night, we were out, and a woman opened an upstairs window and threw the contents of a chamber pot over one of our lads.

Back in north Wales, things weren't much different. Nev had a cup game on one pitch which had a little stream on both sides and a telegraph pole in the centre circle. Unfortunately, one lad had been out the night before and had diarrhoea. He had to keep running down to the stream.

"One of the funniest lads to be around when I got to Everton was John Bailey, our old left-back, who was the butt of a lot of the jokes. Once, he came in and said he'd got an offer to play in South Africa on a great contract. Jim Arnold, our other keeper, said, "What about the apartheid?" He went, "It's all right, it's got three bedrooms."

"Jim was my room-mate, and we came back one night and found there was nothing whatsoever left in it—a couple of players had taken absolutely everything, lamps included. That was typical – I remember trying to get a lift down for dinner once and it was packed with someone's bedroom furniture, "explained Nev.

Pre-seasons could be a particularly ripe time for mischief.

"At one place in Germany, I got a knock on my room at 10 o'clock one night. It was Mark Ward asking me, "Are you coming for breakfast?" I said, "What are you on about? It's 10 at night." I looked into the room he shared with Mo Johnson, and they'd been wrestling and had broken all the slats in their beds. Mo's was lying there, but you could only see his head because his mattress had collapsed in the middle and was now banana-shaped. They'd been out and hadn't a clue what time it was.

I still remember Wardy's first day at the club when Kevin Sheedy and Kevin Ratcliffe wound him up, telling him I loved being chipped. I hated it. It used to drive me mad, so when he did it, I chased him and hit him so hard I broke one of his ribs. I didn't like the fact that the same players wouldn't have the bollocks to do it in a proper game.

It's fair to say I wasn't exactly a saint – I went to the kitman when we were on tour in Sweden once, and when I saw there was no kit, I just walked out in my boots, gloves and underpants. The problem was, I'd not anticipated that there'd be a crowd of people there watching us.

Sheeds was probably the most cutting player I've shared a dressing room with, but everyone could hold their own. Dressing rooms were hard places then. That said, think about the stick you got if you made a mistake in front of tens of thousands of people – and those lads closed ranks when anyone had a go at you.

One of my favourite wind-ups came when Martin Keown joined Everton in 1989. We were going to the Far East for 10 days on a summer tour, and Pat Nevin and I told him: "It's great when you're away because the club pays your mortgage for you, they get someone to go round and cut your grass and wash your car. You must surely have had that in your contract." So we told him to go and see Colin Harvey, our manager, immediately. Martin knocked on Colin's door, and needless to say, he got pretty short shrift.

You also said funny things in the heat of the moment. Once at Chelsea, when Howard Kendall was back at the club for his third spell, he called out to Tony Thomas, one of our squad players, "Tony, get ready to go on in a minute," but Tony never moved. Five minutes later, he said, "Tony, I told you to get ready." Tony went, "Gaffer, I'm in my suit, I'm not even a sub!"

Nothing beats the Wales set-up for that kind of thing. For one game against Iceland in 1984, we didn't have enough substitutes. "Ah, just the man, have you got your boots with you?" said our manager, Mike England. Jeff had stopped for a pint and a pie on the way in, but Mike still made him a sub. After half an hour, Jeremy Charles pulled his hamstring and so on went Jeff in central defence.

Another time we were out in Malta, and Bobby Gould's assistant Graham Williams took us up to this room for a pre-match meal. It was lovely food, so we all started tucking in until this woman rushed in, shouting, "What are you doing in here? This is a wedding; get out! "

There were schoolboy pranks too. When we had Mike Smith in charge, with Dave Williams as his assistant, they were really serious people. Before travelling to play

Germany, we met up in London, and Mike said, "Be down in 10 minutes, we're going to watch a video." Before they came in, Dean Saunders and I switched the video to a porn film, so we're all sat there and there are all these girls in the bath with this fella. Dean piped up, "Look Mike, there's Klinsmann in the bath!" After what felt like an age, Mike turned round to Dave and said, "This isn't the right one!"

Big Nev made an infamous defender-of-the-downtrodden appearance as a mentor on Michael Owen's Soccer Skills, which has become a viral sleeper-hit since resurfacing online years later.

And while Southall desperately tries to teach his tiny 13-year-old charge, 'Jamie', the ins-and-outs of goalkeeping, while Owen—a then-England international considered to be the world's best striker—inexplicably and gleefully gives Jamie no chance with any of his efforts.

Noticing the boy's increasing crushing humiliation on national television, Southall valiantly comes to his aid.

"Geeeet in theeeere!" Owen yelps, wheeling away in celebration, having beaten Jamie at his far post yet again.

"Well done, he's 13." Nev replies, in a magnificently piercing jibe that the show's editors thankfully decided to save from the cutting room floor—a real measure of the man.

Chapter 31
Timeline

Born 16 September 1958
1973–1974 Llandudno Town
1974–1976 Bangor City
1976–1979 Conwy United
1979–1980 Winsford United
1979–80 Winsford United F.C. Player of the Year
1980–1981 Bury
1980–81 Bury F.C. Player of the Year
1980–81 Bury F.C. Young Player of the Year
1981–1998 Everton
1982–1997 WALES
1983 Port Vale (loan)
1984 FA Charity Shield winners medal in 1984,
1984 FA Cup winners medal in 1984
1984–1985 First Division championship medal
1985 FA Charity Shield winners medal
1985 European Cup Winners' Cup medal in
1985 Voted FWA Footballer of the Year
1986–1987 First Division championship medal
1995 FA Cup winners medal
1995 FA Charity Shield winners medal
1995 BBC Wales Sports Personality of the Year
1995 In Search of Perfection Paperback was launched
1996 Appointed a Member of the Order of the British Empire for his services to football.
1997–1998 Southend United (loan)
1997 Everton Blues: Paperback was launched
1998 Stoke City (loan)
1998 Stoke City
1998 Doncaster Rovers
1998–2000 Torquay United
1998–99 Torquay United F.C. Player of the Year
1998 named as one of the Football League 100 Legends
1999 Huddersfield Town (loan)
1999 Wales (caretaker manager)

2000 Bradford City
2001 York City
2001 Rhyl
2001 Shrewsbury Town
2001 Dover Athletic
2001–2002 Shrewsbury Town
2001–2002 Manager at Dover Athletic
2001 The Weekend Warrior: A Comprehensive Guide for Coaching 8 to 10 Year Olds Paperback was launched
2002 Dagenham & Redbridge
2004–2005 Manager at Hastings United
2004 voted as Everton's all-time cult hero
2009 Margate (caretaker manager)
2009 COCO & CO FC LIMITED
2012 Mentor - Ashford Special School in Kent
2012 The Binman Chronicles Paperback was launched
2014 Teaching Assistant - Canolfan Yr Afon
2020 Social Media Takeover
2020 Mind Games: The Ups and Downs of Life and Football Paperback was launched
2022 90 minutes with Neville Southall

References

Mind Games: The Ups and Downs of Life and Football
By Neville Southall
www.amazon.co.uk

Neville Southall: The Binman Chronicles
By Neville Southall, James Corbett
www.amazon.co.uk

Everton Blues: A Premier League Diary
By Neville Southall, Ric George
www.amazon.co.uk

In Search of Perfection
By Neville Southall
www.amazon.co.uk

The Weekend Warrior: A Comprehensive Guide for Coaching 8 to 10 Year Olds
By Neville Southall, David Griffiths, Mick Court
www.goodreads.com

90 Mins with Neville Southall
Podcasts
www.linktr.ee/90minswithnev

Book Neville Southall
After Dinner Speaking
Contact: Sharron Elkabas
+44 (0)207 234 9455

Mersey Memorabilia
www.merseymemorabilia.com

The People's Place,
The People's Hub,
Spellow Lane,

500 metres from Goodison Park.

Information for sex workers
http://www.shinewomen.co.uk/

Rainbow Toffees
Everton's LGBT supporters' group

Football For Change
www.footballforchange.org.uk

JUST A BALL GAME?
www.justaballgame.co.uk

www.lgbt.foundation/sexworkpostcovid